Contemporary Science

Contemporary Science

50 Science Essays for Students

Pallava Bagla

PRABHAT PRAKASHAN
ISO 9001: 2008 Publishers

Published by
PRABHAT PRAKASHAN
4/19 Asaf Ali Road,
New Delhi-110 002 (INDIA)
Tele : +91-11-23289777
e-mail: prabhatbooks@gmail.com

ISBN 978-93-5266-719-2
CONTEMPORARY SCIENCE
by Pallava Bagla

Edition
First, 2018

Price
₹ 500.00 (Rupees Five Hundred only)

Printed at
R-Tech Offset Printers, Delhi

Dr. Malayattil Venugopal,

my sounding board, a gentle giant and eternal student of science who flew into eternity in 2016, and to the hard working Indian scientists who toil endless hours for almost no personal gains, to make India healthy, wealthy and wise!

Preface

In the twenty first century science and technology have become an integral part of our daily lives, everything we touch or use has benefitted at some point or the other from the sweat put in by someone who toiled long hours in laboratory. Yet at the same time obscurantism, superstition and belief in myths continue to dominate our lives.

This paradox is what makes India so very interesting, literally a cauldron of ideas and that is where I waded in by penning these short topical essays on science on topics that to my opinion would interest any general lay reader and especially students who are preparing to enter the job market.

As India enters the seventieth year of its independence it is an opportune time to reflect how well have we done as a country in reaching the fruits of science and technology to the masses. Most recently Chandrayaan-1, India's maiden foray to the moon in 2008 and Mangalyaan in 2013, India's maiden mission to mars became household names and brought to the forefront how much Indians love their scientists.

But go back a little say about 5 decades ago and the country was struggling with famines and even food was in short supply living on food handouts that came in ship loads as food aid from United States of America was the only means of survival a demeaning phrase was coined living 'ship to mouth'. Today thanks to inputs by our hard working agriculture scientists India is a net exporter of food grains.

According to a study by the Ministry of Agriculture and Farmer's Welfare between 1951 and 2014 thanks to the Green Revolution the country increased the production of foodgrains by 5 times, horticultural crops by 9.5 times, fish hauls by 12.5 times, milk production by 7.8 times and output of eggs 39 times. None of this would have been possible had not the governments not invested in the S&T infrastructure and had not the ever obliging Indian citizens not adopted the modern practices.

India is still considered a developing country and this generation is paying the price of all the infra-structure development that is taking place be it nasty air pollution, to lack of adequate health care facilities in rural India to a shortage of trained scientists who can propel India to become the so called 'golden bird it once used to be'.

In this fast changing world where India is growing rapidly the need for students who have a great grounding in science and technology is almost a prerequisite. These essays written in a simple language offers a basic understanding of contemporary scientific issues.

While all effort has been made to keep facts as accurate as possible but sometimes research overtakes writing and all errors if any are the authors who himself continues to be a student of science.

—Pallava Bagla

Acknowledgements

A book like this reflecting contemporary developments in science and technology got its genesis from the weekly contribution I make to the Press Trust of India (PTI) the country's most trusted news agency. I am beholden to Mr. M.K. Razdan the then Chief Executive Officer of PTI and its long serving Editor-in-Chief who gratefully took me on-board as columnist even though news agencies seldom employ columnists. Mr. V S Chandrasekar and Mr. Sudhakar Nair both ably guided me and encouraged to continue penning my weekly features. I am also thankful to Mr. Zafri Nofil and Mr. Netra Pal Sharma who anchored my weekly submissions taking it both to the vast English and Hindi audiences.Thankful also to Mr. Vijay Joshi and Mr. Venky Venkatesh who continue to repose faith in my writings.

I have enjoyed the faith of several science ministers just to name a few Dr. Harsh Vardhan, DrJitendra Singh, and Mr. Kapil Sibal and to the legions of able techno-crats who have led the Indian science ministries. India is rather unique that heads of Indian government science departments are invariably leading scientists, a clear acknowledgement of the deep faith the country has in its boffins.

I am a multi-media person and being Science Editor for New Delhi Television there are many in that ocean of knowledge housed at the 'Archana Arcade' who shaped many of my writings just to name a few of my colleagues who taught me something Sonia Singh, ManikaRaikwar,

Chetan Bhattacharjee, Nidhi Razdan, Sunil Saini, Ravish Kumar, Vishnu Som Amitabh Reevi, Deepak Kumar Choubey, Ajmal Jami, Narendra Gudavalli, Suparna Singh, Nilanjana Bhaduri-Jha, Anindita Sanyal,C. Sudhakar, Ratan Bharadwaj, Subrat Nanda, Madhusudan Srinivas. And the energetic pioneers of Indian television news Prannoy Roy and Radhika Roy who judged me to be good enough to be their science editor.

Being a dedicated still photographer I am thankful to my editors at Getty Images who sift through my contributions taking it to the world.

At Science magazine where I have been a correspondent for a long time my warmest thanks to Richard Stone. Thanks are also due to Mahendra Vyas, R.K. Tuli and Bhavna and Manish Upneja.

I am grateful to my family who gives me the time and space to communicate science with passion for which I am eternally obliged to Subhadra Menon, Nayantara and Ashwat Bagla, Gunjan and Smita Bagla, Aviral and Anshika Bagla, Madhavi Menon, Mandakini Menon, Siddhartha Menon and Radhika Ranawat Menon and my childhood friends Dr. Harsh Rastogi and Dr. Samir Govil.

To Sushma Kerketa and Maninder Singh, my special thanks.

Last and not the least to Facebook, Twitter and Instagram where I run a daily photo blog titled 'Enjoy Nature' and platforms where I get the most bouquets and brickbats in these times of the exploding social media where instant gratification is the norm.

Contents

Preface 7
Acknowledgements 9

AGRICULTURE

1. Magic Millet: Poor Man's Cereal gets an Enrichment Boost to Cure Anaemia 19
2. Wealth from Waste: A Novel Indian Biotech Solution that Efficiently Convert Agri-Waste into Alcohol 22
3. A Miracle Rice that Saved India from Famines! 27

ASTRONOMY

4. Go, Ligo-India Go where no One has gone before! A Nobel Prize Awaits 33

BIOLOGY

5. Is Ganga Water Special because of an Enigmatic X-Factor, Government Launches Intensive Search to Resolve the Mystery of this 'Brahma Dravya'! 39

SCIENCE

6. A Ticking Time Bomb, waiting for the next big Earthquake Scientists try to Decipher Signatures of Past Temblors 47

7. India: A Leader in Tsunami Warnings 52

8. Science gets a tight embrace in the Modi government 58

ENERGY

9. Is Solar Power the Real Solution to India's Energy Crisis? 65

ENVIRONMENT

10. Everyday Plastics Spell Doom for the Oceans 71

11. Beef eating is Bad for Environment. Shun Beef Save the Planet say Experts! 75

12. In a Global First, the World Bank goes to a Zoo in India! 79

13. New Delhi choking! root cause Stems from a Deep Crisis in Indian Agriculture! 83

14. Killer Air: Solution to Pollution is not Dilution but better Public Transportation 88

HEALTH

15. The Weight Loss Paradox: Low Fat Diets are no better than High Fat Diets in the Long-Term! 93

16. WHO urges India to be Vigilant, as a New Deadly 'Camel Virus' shakes the Soul of Seoul City 96

17. Mobile Phones, White Coats and Neckties all part of a Doctor's Attire Spread Dangerous Infections 100

18. India could be Hit by a Tsunami of Obesity! 104

19. What ails India? A New Study finds on any given Day about 35 Million Indians could be Unwell! 108

20. ISRO's Rocket Technology to power Human Hearts 112

21. Health Ministry's Own Survey Projects a Bleak Picture 116

22. Taming a Tiny Terrorist called TB, Indian Scientists provide New Insights for Drug Discovery 120

23. Failing Antibiotics: The World Wakes up to the Worst Horror! 124

INTERNATIONAL

24. Burgeoning Indo-US relations: Denial of Visas to Scientists remains A Big Thorn in the Flesh 131

25. Amazing Molecules with Life-Saving Properties discovered Literally from the Cold by Indian Biologists 136

26. 'Human Sacrifice' in Shiva's abode inside the Kingdom of God Particles. Irrational behaviour by European Scientists riles India! 141

NUCLEAR

27. Presence of Radioactivity in Steel could dent the 'Make in India' Effort 147

28. Waste to Wealth: BARC Pioneers New Life Saving Radiation Technology 151

29. Kakrapar Atomic Plant Leak Exposes a 'Mysterious' chink in Armour; Indian Nuclear Plants need urgent Systemic Safety Review 155

30. Fourteen Year 'Vanvas' ends in Kudankulam bringing Cheers & Tears at India's Secretive Nuclear Establishment 160

31. At Pokharan Indian, designed planes & missiles show firepower, DRDO quietly exults 166

PERSONALITY

32. 'Kalam Island' should be the New Name of Wheeler Island, the 'Karam Bhoomi' of India's Missile Man A.P.J. Abdul Kalam 173

33. Mother Teresa was a Living 'God' Why Attribute Irrational Miracles to Her for Granting Her the Status of a Saint 178

34. M.G.K. Menon a Remarkable Polymath Scientist Leaves a behind Big Void! 183

POLICY

35. Coming soon a Never before Reactor; Friendship Satellite and a New Universal Polio Vaccine: Big-Ticket Sci-Tech Push Expected in 2016 191

36. On Its Platinum Jubilee an aging CSIR cries for Renewal, but is Forced to Behave Likes a Glorified ITI! 196

POLITICS

37. Modi Sarkar Anniversary: Mangalyaan brought Cheers; the Monsoon could bring Tears; while Scientists live in Fear 205

38. Modi's Gift a Mangalyaan in Every Hand! 210

39. Back to the Future from Food Rationing to Cash Rationing! 214

40. Israel Prime Minister Benjamin Netanyahu's 'entrepreneurial' advice to PM Narendra Modi on 'start up India, stand up India' 218

SPACE

41. America Looks to Partner in India's Quest for Deep Space Exploration! As India goes Planet Hunting, ISRO Eyeing Venus, Mars and Asteroid 225
42. India and China set Their Eyes on a Joint Satellite Constellation even as Pakistan bails out of SAARC Satellite 229
43. ISRO's Big Leap Embarks on Launching an Indian Space Shuttle! 234
44. ISRO's Century Emboldens it to Embrace Private Sector. But is the Love Affair One Sided? 238
45. ISRO in Service of the Indian Soldier and the Indian War Machine 244
46. ISRO's French Connection 250
47. Moon shot Politics: Will an Indian start-up 'Tea Indus' beat ISRO in Planting India's Flag on the Moon? 255
48. Troubles from Neighbours make India and Israel Forge Friendly Ties in Space 260
49. Touching Lives : ISRO's space technology can save lives of soldiers at the Siachin Glacier 263
50. Big gains for ISRO under Modi. 'Ache Din and a Naya Savera' for the Indian space community as NAVIC was navigated into place 268

AGRICULTURE

1

Magic Millet: Poor Man's Cereal gets an Enrichment Boost to Cure Anaemia

Indian scientists have bred a novel nutritious variety of millet, very rich in iron. A global clinical trial has now proved that if this 'magic millet' is used to feed children, incidence of iron deficiency or anaemia can be reduced dramatically. The Ministry of Agriculture has applauded this development and the iron-rich pearl millet variety is being adopted in the national effort to tackle malnutrition.

Pearl millet or *bajra* is sometimes called a poor man's cereal since as affluence increases populations generally tend to eat more wheat and rice, yet in India, some 50 million people still use *bajra* as their staple source of food. The International Crops Research Institute for the Semi-Arid Tropics (ICRISAT) in Hyderabad bred a new hybrid variety of Pearl Millet called '*Dhanshakti*' that has almost 11% more iron than the traditional parent varieties. According to ICRISAT, the new variety not only gives a better yield but also provides more fodder. Mahalingam Govindraj, a plant breeder at ICRISAT who works on this new selection, says: "The variety has been bred using traditional methods and no genetic modification technology has been used". ICRISAT along with a private seed company Nirmal Seeds are launching major initiative, which estimates that by 2018 some 1.17 million farming households will have access to iron-rich pearl millet.

Pearl millets are very hardy plants and can survive in rain-fed harsh farms; the only watering these plants require is during the sowing when the seeds are simply broadcast by the farmers.

While laboratory experiments suggested that '*Dhanshakti*' variety was indeed bio-enriched for iron content, but the proof of the pudding was if it could help ameliorate iron deficiencies. Towards that scientists from the Cornell University and the S.N.D.T. Women's University in Mumbai conducted a randomized clinical trial on 246 children in Ahmednagar district of Maharashtra. School-going children in the age group 12-16 years were provided as part of mid-day meal '*bajra bhakri*'s' a type of *chapatti*. The six-month trial found that eating iron-rich millet was able to reverse iron deficiency in six months and in four months, the iron levels showed marked improvement. According to the study published in *The Journal of Nutrition*, "those children who were iron deficient at the start and ate iron-rich pearl millet '*bhakri*' were 1.6 times more likely to have resolved their iron deficiency compared with those who ate *bhakri* made from the ordinary pearl millet". A simple solution to a complex problem.

Hidden Hunger is a Huge Problem

A recent report by the UN's Food and Agriculture Organisation finds that India is home to 194.6 million undernourished people, the highest in the world and India is ranked 112 among 141 nations with reference to the Child Development Index. Last year's assessment by the National Food Security Mission of India says that 42% of children in India are underweight and 58% of children are stunted by two years of age. It reveals a startling number that 70% of Indian women and children have serious nutritional deficiencies like iron, zinc and calcium.

According to the US National Institutes of Health, "An

estimated 1.6 billion people worldwide are anaemic, and iron deficiency (ID) is the leading cause of anaemia. Even mild anaemia can adversely impact cognitive performance, behaviour, and physical growth of children, and physical work and cognitive performance in adults". According to the Women and Child Development Ministry, "It is estimated that about 20% to 40% of maternal deaths in India are due to anaemia; India contributes to about 50% of global maternal deaths due to anaemia." A 2009 estimate by P.V. Kotecha working with the US-AID Micronutrient Project in India, "Nearly 73 million children below the age of three (79%) suffer from varying degrees of anaemia, and over 50 million suffer from moderate-to-severe anaemia." The biofortified pearl millet offers a ready solution, today multigrain breads and *'atta'* is gaining popularity even in big cities where health foods are now fashionable.

A big breakthrough using simple tools. Julia L. Finkelstein, Assistant Professor of Epidemiology and Nutrition, in the Division of Nutritional Sciences, Cornell University who piloted the clinical trial in Maharashtra said the findings from this study demonstrate for the first time that iron biofortified pearl millet can improve levels of iron in the body among school-aged children with greatest potential to benefit among children with the lowest levels of body iron. In addition, individuals with low levels of body iron who are not anaemic can also benefit from consumption of iron biofortified pearl millet. Emphasizing that "This is the first study to demonstrate a positive effect of consuming iron biofortified pearl millet on improving body iron levels in this age group."

The Indian Government has also launched ₹ 200 crore 'nutri farms scheme', through which such nutritionally-enhanced crops can be grown in districts that have high prevalence of malnutrition all in the hope of reducing hidden hunger.

June 13, 2015

□

2

Wealth from Waste: A Novel Indian Biotech Solution that Efficiently Convert Agri-Waste into Alcohol

Agricultural waste is becoming a mammoth problem for India, not knowing what to do with the stubble, many Indian farmers especially in granary of the country simply burn it after harvest. This not only causes air pollution but also even causes a huge plume of air pollution over many cities a little after the harvest season. Now Indian scientists supported by the Department of Biotechnology (DBT) have come up with a nifty solution that using a biorefinery converts this waste into value-added alcohol, which, can then be used as clean biofuel or blended to make spirits.

NASA has recorded this burning of biomass from its satellites and American scientists say the black carbon released by this crop waste burning is leading to the wasting of Himalayan glaciers. This can easily be mitigated if agri-waste can be converted into clean biofuel.

This month India's Science Minister Dr. Harsh Vardhan inaugurated the first demonstration plant located within the premises of India Glycol Limited in Kashipur that converts almost any kind of agricultural organic waste into alcohol. The technology for this plant has been made by the

Institute of Chemical Technology (ICT), Mumbai at a cost of ₹ 40 crores and thereafter the demonstration plant has been made at a cost of ₹ 35 crores with support from the Department of Biotechnology.

Making alcohol from biological material is not new, but till date most of the ethanol is made using sugar-cane, corn or some such food material and is called first-generation ethanol. Since the Kashipur, plant utilizes purely agricultural waste it is referred to as second-generation (2G) ethanol. Dr. K. Vijay Raghavan, Secretary of the Department of Biotechnology says "This is the most suited technology for India since to make the biofuel the feedstock does not compete with food".

According to the DBT, "This Kashipur plant comes at a time when the country struggles to meet the mandate of 5% blending of renewable biofuel in both ethanol and diesel. While diesel biofuel blending is near zero, the petrol blending today stands at an overall of about 3% in the form of first generation or molasses based 1G-ethanol. With an annual requirement of about 5000 million litres, the oil companies will starve for ethanol as the current total installed capacity of 1G-ethanol stands at about 2650 million litres. In such a scenario, the targets of 10% blending by 2017 and 20% by 2020 look remote unless second generation or agriculture waste-based ethanol, i.e. second generation or 2G-ethanol production technologies get going. However, the 2G-ethanol production technologies have struggled world-wide to be economically and technologically viable despite more than 100 pilot plants and about 10 demonstration and commercial plants erected and commissioned over the last decade."

The Kashipur plant made as public-private partnership or PPP model is actually a series of big bioreactors. The plant was utilizing wheat and bagasse-agri waste at this time. The dry waste is pushed into the plant and then using chemicals it is rapidly converted into slurry, this is then easy to pump around in the three-storey high plant where the key reaction is performed using cellulose enzymes that convert the cellulose the main organic component of bio-waste into sugars. Thereafter, the enzyme is recovered back using membrane technology and the expensive imported enzyme is then recycled back into the plant. Subsequently, the sugars are passed through a broth of yeasts, which convert it into ethanol.

Mr. U.S. Bhartiya, chairman-cum-managing director of India Glycols Limited says "This plant can easily be replicated and is an apt solution for India's huge biomass problem". Today according to Bhartiya for every 1000 kilograms of agri waste that is pumped into the plant it generates about 300 litres of alcohol. The water that is used in the plant can also be recycled back making it a highly green technology option feels Bhartiya. This demonstration plant has a capacity of 10 tons of biomass per day.

According to DBT, "The demonstration plant at India Glycols Limited built indigenously as a continuous automated plant assumes considerable significance. The technology and the plant, projected to be capable of converting any biomass feedstock like wheat straw, rice straw, bagasse, cotton stalk, bamboo, etc. to alcohol in less than 24 hours, if successfully operated and scaled-up will establish India as a major global technology provider in the arena of renewables and reduction in carbon-emissions besides effecting considerable savings in import of crude oil."

According to Dr. Arvind Lali the Head of the DBT-ICT Centre in Mumbai, they have already designed plants of 250 ton per day and 500 ton per day capacities and is confident that the technology with the lowest capital and operating costs that would allow 2G-alcohol to be produced and sold at competitive price. The cost of litre of ethanol from the Indian 2G technology is pegged at ₹ 25 per litre.

The Indian plant compared to similar plants like those by DuPont converts waste to alcohol five times more efficiently. All the other overseas plants take several days to process the waste into a biofuel, whereas the Kashipur plant according to engineers at IGL takes just one day. This efficiency is because of custom-made pre-treatment of waste, which converts it into slurry unlike, that foreign plants that push solid material through their plants, said the in-charge of the IGL plant.

Dr. Harsh Vardhan, Union Cabinet Minister for Science, Technology and Earth Sciences said "Second generation ethanol being produced from so-called agricultural waste which becomes an asset to the farmer, it helps the contentious issue of climate change and global warming, it helps us to reduce carbon emissions." This also offers a suitable solution to the air pollution caused due to stubble burning from fields in northern India. However, there are some who worry that in a country with a vast cattle and livestock population widespread deployment of this technology could hurt traditional livelihoods. However, others say as of now the need is to contain this unnecessary burning.

From the raw feedstock, the 2G-ethanol plant generates a third of it as lignin, this lignin as of now being used as fuel, but according to well-known chemist M.M. Sharma who is associated with ICT feels this can also be used as raw material to generate carbon black that can be used for making tyres. Sharma even suggests rapidly the plant should be upgraded to manufacture butanol instead of ethanol, which is an even higher value product, and much in demand.

According to estimates by the government, "India's potential for 2G-ethanol production from an estimated availability of non-food and non-fodder agricultural residues stands to be in excess of 300 million tons which if converted can produce nearly 100 million litres of ethanol." A vast treasure trove remains untapped and is almost being wasted, only if this trash is converted to wealth billions of dollars of foreign exchange could be saved by way of averted oil imports and India could get a cleaner air by burning a cleaner biofuel in the form of ethanol.

May 1, 2016

□

3

A Miracle Rice that Saved India from Famines!

Today Indians are forcibly standing in queues as cash is rationed, sixty years ago Indians were also standing in queues as food was rationed. Staple foods, rice and wheat was in short supply people had to stand in serpentine queues to buy a few kilograms of foodgrains. Life indeed was tough.

In fact, most of Asia was on the brink of starvation in the 1950's then came a miracle plant developed by scientists at the International Rice Research Institute (IRRI) in the Philippines that experts say 'changed the world'. This small rice plant called IR-8 doubled the yields and it led to a farming revolution that saved millions of lives. After the World War II and the horrible great Bengal famine that killed nearly 2-3 million people, a miracle was required to save the lives of starving Indians, then came this blade of new grass that helped slowly propel India into a new era of food self-sufficiency.

Rice in the 1950s was a tall plant that gave few grains and was very prone to lodging or falling over and hence a lot of grain used to get spoilt. The need was to have a short robust plant that had many tillers or gran bearing stems. Scientists at IRRI married two strains of rice one from Indonesia and one from Taiwan and thus was born a plant that saved the world called 'IR-8'.

Gurdev Khush a plant geneticist and till recently the chief rice breeder at IRRI who played a huge role in making IR-8 the 'miracle plant', says usual plant breeding offered incremental small one to two per cent increases in yield but IR-8 offered an astronomical doubling of the yield. According to IRRI, "The IR-8 was the first offspring of these intense breeding efforts. It was a semi-dwarf rice and was the result of a cross between Peta, a tall vigorous variety, and Dee-geo-woo-gen, a dwarf variety".

Dr. M.S. Swaminathan dubbed as the Father of the Indian green revolution and former Director General of IRRI said "IR made global history as the yield ceiling was broken." He adds that it is the Indian farmer who was the real saviour as they are always willing to learn and adapt to new technologies as long as the costs are economical.

The seeds of this 'miracle rice' were widely distributed free of cost and without any patent protection in Philippines, India and other parts of Asia. The plant was immediately lapped up by the farmers in East Asia. In Vietnam and adjoining countries, the new rice variety came to be called 'Honda rice', since the profits from a single crop were enough for farmers to buy Honda motorcycles.

In India, a young farmer Nekkanti Subba Rao, from Andhra Pradesh was the first to embrace the new variety. IRRI's official magazine *Rice Today* recounts that "In 1967, Mr. Subba Rao tested IR-8 on his farm and supervised its first large-scale demonstration and multiplication—on about 2,000 hectares near his home village of Atchanta—following instructions from the Government of India. The next year, IR-8 was planted on 1,600 hectares in his village and the rest was history, with the seeds soon being distributed throughout the country. So, in addition to being called *Dhaan Pandit* (rice expert) by his neighbours, he is also known by the moniker 'Mr. IR-8, "which still resonates with many Indian farmers to this day".

Now in his eighties Rao celebrated the golden jubilee of that first embrace with IR-8 last month which he asserts "Changed the fate of a starving nation to a country with an overflowing godown". Rao recalls that even though IR-8 doubled the yield it did not become the consumers and housewives delight, in India as it had a short sticky grains. Indians love longer non-sticky grains and he says genetic tinkering of the original IR-8 variety by Indian scientists led to the development of new varieties called Jaya and Padma that changed the whole scenario of rice cultivation in India.

Samarendu Mohanty a social scientist at IRRI estimates that between 1966 when IR-8 was first introduced to the world to 2015, this single rice variety and its direct progeny may have contributed about 190 million tons of paddy. Undoubtedly a humongous quantity which T. Mohapatra, Director General of the Indian Council of Agriculture Research (ICAR) says "Led to a whole new revolution in agriculture".

Khush is one Indian rice breeder whose signatures are seen in almost all varieties of rice grown all over the world since most existent rice varieties carry one gene or the other that has been tinkered upon by Khush and his team.

Recalling with immense pride on his association with rice breeding Khush says in the 1960s every year, India was importing some ten million tons of rice, today India is the second largest producer of rice and actually exports over ten million tons of rice to the world, 'no mean achievement' explains Khush.

How IR-8 changed the world can be estimated by the fact that between 1960 and 2016 the population of the India has tripled and in the same time frame thanks to IR-8 and its progeny the rice production has increased more than five times. "Widespread famines are a thing of the past for India", asserts Khush.

As one top scientist from ICAR said "Thank God we

are only standing in queues to get cash and that worst nightmare of the last century of living from ship to mouth" is thankfully behind us. A blade of grass that saved and made India!

December 18, 2016

□

ASTRONOMY

4

Go, Ligo-India Go where no One has gone before! A Nobel Prize Awaits

Two American detectors created history when they heard a blast from the past, if all goes as per plan, India could be the home for a third similar listening post that would help unravel deep secrets of the universe.

The discovery of past murmurs from a 1.3 billion old cataclysmic collision of two black holes was heard by two super sophisticated detectors located in America; this sound of merging black holes led a team of over a 1000 scientists to discover what are called gravitation waves, a true perturbation in the fabric of space and time. It is hailed as the discovery of a century. It also proves what the genius physicist Albert Einstein had theoretically predicted almost a century ago.

There is a huge India connect to this discovery, there are many Indian institutions like the Raman Research Institute, Bengaluru among others who have directly contributed to this landmark finding. However, if only the Indian Government had acted in a timely manner, India could well have heard the same murmurs as well. There is a scientific plan pending since 2011 for setting up a third detector and the first outside the USA, in India. The chirp which heralded the arrival of gravitation waves could well have turned into a roar, had the Indian government been quick in its decision-making. While the United Progressive Alliance (UPA) Government led by Prime Minister Manmohan Singh gave an in-principle clearance in 2014 but it failed to allocate funds for this mega-science project.

In contrast seizing the opportunity of this huge discovery, the space buff in Prime Minister Narendra Modi within twenty minutes of the global announcement gave a statement that has gladdened the Indian scientific community. Modi said "Historic detection of gravitational waves opens up new frontier for understanding of universe! Immensely proud, that Indian scientists played an important role in this challenging quest. Hope to move forward to make even bigger contribution with an advanced gravitational wave detector in the country." If his last sentence that makes the Indian astronomy community feel buoyant that the dream of having a third Laser Interferometer Gravitation Wave Observatory (LIGO) detector in India could well be a reality.

The global community is already pitching for it, well-known Astrophysicist Prof. Shrinivas R. Kulkarni from California Institute of Technology (CALTECH), USA one of the host institutes of the global effort says "Sir Modi Ji, please allocate money for this very important Indian LIGO project and I know it is under consideration, this will be money well spent. It will uplift physics departments across the country, lots of new technologies, precision laser and powerful laser technology could flow to India. It will globalise Indian science."

It was only in 2014 that India decided to log into detecting the most elusive of all characters of mass, space and time, the gravity waves. Known to exist since Albert Einstein postulated them in 1916 as part of the theory of general relativity but they have been difficult to unravel till this week's landmark discovery.

Speaking in the midst of 8000 scientists in 2014 at the

inaugural session of the Indian Science Congress in Jammu, then Indian Prime Minister Manmohan Singh surprised many by saying "In the gravitational wave experiment, India intends to host the third detector."

Special giant laser detectors operating since 2001 in USA at Hanford in Washington and Livingston in Louisiana, work over time detect these waves. Yet the global astronomical community wanted another detector to be placed far away from the ones in America. Postulating that through this triangulation the source of the gravitation waves as they emerged in the cosmos could be better pinpointed.

Funded by the US National Science Foundation and spearheaded by Caltech a $ 140 million Laser Interferometer Gravitational Wave Observatory (LIGO) is proposed to be placed in India, the location is yet to be finalized, but sites in Rajasthan and Maharashtra have been surveyed. The detector would be an L-shaped vacuum tube which extends four kilometres on each arm through which a high intensity laser beam is bounced back and forth between mirrors and variations and perturbations in the light caused by gravitation waves are detected. The Indian project called LiGo-India or also referred sometimes as IndiGo would be almost identical to the detectors that detected the gravitation waves on September 14, 2014 in America.

The global community got very excited by this Indian announcement especially since an earlier effort to put a similar observatory in Australia failed in 2012, as the host country could not rustle up the funding.

Hope has been awakened since Prime Minister Narendra Modi has logged into the LIGO-India project and gotten excited as it could a shining example of a 'make in India' effort.

Scientists familiar with the project suggest that the Indian Government is likely to commit about ₹ 1000 crores funding for the Indian LIGO effort over the next 15 years, it is being spearheaded by the Department of Atomic Energy.

Some researchers have always worried that finding a vacant plot of land low on ambient noise that can house the giant detector in a country with high population density having a total population of 1.25 billion is going to be a big challenge.

Countering the nay sayers Ratan Kumar Sinha, nuclear engineer and then Chairman Atomic Energy Commission, Mumbai told the Science magazine "LIGO will bring some of the best international and Indian astrophysicists to work on the Indian soil on a very exciting area of research aiming to verify a very important aspect of Einstein's general theory of relativity. The investment of $ 201 million will directly benefit our industry and our student community". India already has a lead.

Indian scientists like Sanjeev Dhurandhar and Satya Prakash both then at the Inter University Center for Astronomy and Astrophysics, Pune more than a decade ago deduced the algorithms or the mathematical formula based on which the signal could be detected from the background noise. Not an easy achievement since the 'chirp' of the merging black holes was heard for just few milliseconds in years of observation that led to the discovery of gravitation waves. In all about 37 Indian scientists and about 23 non-resident Indian scientists have contributed on this big discovery. Kulkarni says "India's contribution to the detection of gravitation waves should be recognised in a Nobel Prize when it is awarded".

Meanwhile the Indian scientific community hopes that the Indian Cabinet will clear the proposal at the earliest and the Finance Minister allocates some funds in the upcoming budget. Till then keep listening to the rare celestial music of merging black holes.

February 14, 2016

□

BIOLOGY

5

Is Ganga Water Special because of an Enigmatic X-Factor, Government Launches Intensive Search to Resolve the Mystery of this 'Brahma Dravya'!

Is there a mysterious X-factor that makes waters of the River Ganges special? Nothing has been conclusively found even though many theories have swirled around for a long time. In what seems a final push the Prime Minister Narendra Modi-led government is seeking to finally resolve the mystery. A huge multi institution effort costing over ₹ 150 crores is underway to scientifically resolve the enigma of this so-called *'Brahma Dravya'*.

J.P. Nadda, Union Minister for Health and Family Welfare has assured all support for this research including financial assistance to further investigate the claim made through various existing research and studies that the waters of Ganga River have medicinal properties, which destroy various kinds of bacteria and microbes, in order to use it for holistic human health.

Ganga is undoubtedly one of India's holiest rivers and for eons its waters are known to possess some so-called 'magical' properties that ensures that its waters don't spoil even when stored for years. This is often called the self-cleansing property of the river.

River Ganga is the lifeline for about 300-400 million people who reside in its basin which is over 2500 kilometres in length. Yet today the Ganga is one of the most polluted rivers of the world with water pollution levels at places thousands of times the permissible levels. Yet the devout take a dip in the river unmindful of the toxic soup they immerse into.

Many theories have been proposed on what could lead to *Gangajal* being 'special'. Medicinal plants growing on the banks of the river are thought to impart the special properties. The presence of special 'killer microbes', that knockout bacteria, is another idea that finds traction. The presence of some special radioactive elements that help Ganga remaining clean is also conjectured. The high decibel sound waves that emanate from the gongs and bells that ring out on the banks of the river are also thought to be involved. Despite these ideas, conclusive evidence has never been found.

This week more than 200 leading scientists gathered at the All India Institute of Medical Sciences (AIIMS), New Delhi to deliberate on the 'Non-Putrefying Properties of Ganga Water'. It included civil engineers, microbiologists, botanists, virologists, biotechnologists, and even cultural leaders from the Rashtriya Swayamsewak Sangh (RSS) all thinking aloud how to resolve the mystery that has dogged the river for centuries.

Speaking at the meeting, Shri Krishna Gopal described as an environmentalist who deeply understands the Ganga drew upon the studies and research conducted on the exclusive cleansing property of the Ganga water. He pointed to the references from the *Akbarnama* and the 1896 reports of the British bacteriologist Ernest Hanbury Hankin, to state that the presence of bacteriophage activity had been detected in the river since long. New research needs to be conducted to further renew this claim, he added.

Among all theories it seems the Ministry of Health and Family Welfare and the Clean Ganga Mission seeks to explore deeply is the possibility of the presence of special viruses that kill bacteria. Towards this a ₹ 150 crore study is already underway at the National Environmental Engineering Research Institute (NEERI), Nagpur which has already collected over 150 samples of water and Ganga sediment to analyse its microbiological properties. It will take another six months to complete the study asserts Uma Bharati, Minister for Water Resources, River Development and Ganga Rejuvenation. Further highlighting that despite crores of people taking a dip in the river during numerous religious occasions every year, the river has not led to any pandemic or epidemic. This had to be the consequence of some self-purifying power of the river water, which prevented its deterioration, Bharati stated.

Bharati accepts that the Ganga retains its pristine waters only till near Haridwar after which most of the water is diverted away into irrigation canals and then through much of the stretch in the plains the river is merely a *'nallah'* or sewage drain collecting effluents as it traverses through the Indo-Gangetic plain. Bharati feels the detailed study may unravel the truth of what is really happening in this very holy river. Bharati calls the mysterious X-factor the *'Brahma Dravya'* or 'divine liquid', which may be giving the river its special property.

The new push could easily be dismissed as another push by the ruling National Democratic Alliance (NDA) which has made cleaning up the Ganga as part of its core agenda. So is this an effort by the powerful right-wingers to take foreword a Hindutva agenda? Possibly, but the high profile scientific institutions involved are unlikely to succumb to such pressures. In addition to AIIMS, New Delhi, scientists from the Indian Council of Medical Research (ICMR), New

Delhi; IIT Kanpur and Roorkee; Banaras Hindu University, National Environmental Engineering Research Institute (NEERI), Nagpur and National Botanical Research Institute, Lucknow will be participating in this detailed study. None known for having buckled under political pressure.

Ganga water retains self-purification characteristics even in 16-year-old samples explains Dr. Chandra Shekhar Nautiyal, Director of the National Botanical Research Institute, Lucknow. He says Ganga water has been used from time immemorial for medicinal and ritualistic purposes, as it does not putrefy even after long periods of storage. Nautiyal has studied the Ganga waters for more than a decade and finds that Ganga water is soft and has high level of sulphur content. Presence of bacteriophage against the pathogenic bacteria was observed only in Ganga water, he says.

Leading the current effort Dr. Satish R Wate, Director of NEERI says in most rivers, organic matter usually exhausts a river's available oxygen and then the water starts to putrefy. Nevertheless, in Ganga, an unknown factor acts on the organic matter and bacteria and kills them. Ganga's self-purifying property leads to retaining 25 times more oxygen levels than any other river in the world. Early results from NEERI's work indicate that both the *Gangajal* and the sediment from the river help in the self-cleansing property.

Nadda feels that in a world increasingly fighting various kinds of new and more powerful drug resistant bacteria and germs, such a study, which explores and examines what is it that lends this unique property to the Ganga water that not only cleanses itself by destroying germs and microbes present in it, but also purifies other waters, is worth conducting.

In world looking for viable solutions to contain bacterial infections, which are increasingly becoming multi-drug resistant. If these bacteriophages found in the waters of the

Ganga could be harnessed then may be "*Gangajal* could be used as source of medicine" explains M.C. Misra, Director of AIIMS, who thinks even if it is a long shot it is worth exploring why water from the Ganges does not spoil using today's modern scientific tools to unravel the mystery. On her part, the saffron-clad water resources Minister, Bharati says she is open to accepting the findings of the scientific investigations and asserts that recreating the past glory of the river is her main mission in life. So will the X-factor or the '*Brahma Dravya*' emerge from the depths? None of the scientists are too sure but remain optimistically hopeful.

November 22, 2015

□

SCIENCE

6

A Ticking Time Bomb, Waiting for the Next Big Earthquake Scientists Try to Decipher Signatures of Past Temblors

India is highly vulnerable to earthquakes. According to an estimate by the World Bank in a year, about 1000 small and big earthquakes strike the Indian region. The 6.7 magnitude earthquake that recently struck Imphal in the wee hours of January 3 thankfully did not cause huge number of fatalities, but it should serve as another wake-up call.

The National Disaster Management Authority (NDMA) in an assessment found that almost 59% of India is, 'vulnerable to moderate or severe seismic hazard'. Startlingly, it also found that most buildings in sub-urban areas are "non-engineered and built without adhering to earthquake resistant construction principles-traditional houses are being replaced with modern reinforced cement concrete (RCC) buildings, often without compliance to building codes and bye-laws". The NDMA reports that between 1990 and 2006 India has experienced six major earthquakes that have resulted in deaths of over 23,000 people and caused enormous loss to infrastructure. The NDMA echoes an ominous warning, "very severe earthquakes are likely to occur anytime in the Himalayan region, which could adversely affect the lives of several million people". But a complacent government and civil society does not seem to care much about these forewarnings.

"A time bomb is ticking it is not a question if but when the big great earthquake of over 8 magnitude will strike northern India" asserted Professor C.P. Rajendran a paleo-seismologist at the Jawaharlal Nehru Centre for Advanced Scientific Research (JNCASR), Bengaluru. His concerns were echoed by Harsh Gupta a hugely respected seismologist and former secretary of the Ministry of Earth Sciences who says, "in a way, yes there is a ticking bomb because a great earthquake in Himalayan region is overdue it could occur any time."

Since predicting earthquakes is nearly impossible, scientists try to study the past records to try decipher some clues for future forecasting. According to a recent report by the JNCASR, the central part of the Himalaya is noted for its frequent earthquakes. It becomes crucial to study past earthquakes to understand the pattern of recurrence – how frequently the earthquakes occur, under what conditions. The area also contains many natural limestone caves, which act as sites that preserve imprints of major earthquake events in the area.

"The caves the scientists studied are located close to these faults will also be disturbed because of the ground movements", Rajendran explains. "We chose some caves because they were located between two major Himalayan thrusts [faults]: Main Central Thrust (MCT) and Main Boundary Thrust (MBT). So any major ground shaking associated with earthquake activities linked to these structures will possibly be recorded within the cave in the form of growth anomalies", he added.

The central Indian Himalayas have many natural limestone caves, where water from the roof causes two types of formations to occur. Stalactites are pillars of calcium salts that hang from the roof, and stalagmites, again made of calcium, grow up from the floor of the caves says the report. "The caves get tilted due to earthquakes, and cave formations like stalagmites have to read just their growth trajectories. These changes can be understood from the tilt angles preserved in the body of stalagmites. Another kind of damage expected is related to collapse of cave roofs due to earthquake shaking", explains Rajendran. The width and length of the stalagmite depend on the drip water, the size of the droplet and the distance from the ceiling. Each layer preserved within the stalagmite often acts as a repository of its growth history—something like tree bands that allow us insight into the past.

Each growth band can be dated precisely, explains Rajendran. "Moreover, as many are long lived, for thousands of years, it can give a long-term history of their growth. Both climatic and tectonic signals can be ideally deciphered from them. Deviations from the systematic growth is expected to reflect the ground tilting due to big earthquakes", says Rajendran.

The study of stalagmites gives a tool to go back much deeper into past and in conjunction with geological and geophysical data help us expand databases on earthquake hazard of the Himalayan region reports Rajendran.

Another reason why temblors of high magnitude are expected in northern India is because of the rather unique and peculiar geological history of India. According to the well-accepted theory of plate tectonics which explains the movement over aeons of the continental plates all floating on an ocean of molten magma in the core of the Earth. As a consequence, some 71 million years ago the Indian sub-continent actually started drifting away from Africa moving northwards later it came and collided with the huge Asian landmass. Since then the Indian plate is constantly being pushed under the Asian plate at the rate of about five centimetres every year. This jostling builds up a huge strain deep within the earth starting in a large, almost 2400 kilometre swathe stretching from Afghanistan to Arunachal Pradesh. When this inherent but latent pressure built due to the tectonic wrestling is released, we sense it as earthquakes. The young and restless Himalayas that are still rising annually by about five millimetres epitomize and literally showcase the danger that is hidden and building up deep within the womb of earth. Gupta says, "there is a definite possibility of the great earthquake, of magnitude 8 in the Himalayan region, there is no doubt about it...when it will happen, no one can guess, where it will happen, is also a big question mark".

Each of these earthquakes results from what seismologists call a big rupture that occurs in the crust of the earth, literally a deep shearing of the plates as they rub against each other on the fault line and the pent up stress is released in the form of energy that causes the jolts. According to an estimate published in the reputed American journal *Science* by leading Indian seismologist Vinod K. Gaur at the Indian Institute of Astrophysics' such big earthquakes have a revisit time of almost 500 years. Roger Bilham a top seismologist from the Department of Geological Sciences, University of Colorado in Boulder, USA says "more important today, is that less than half of the Himalayas has ruptured", which essentially means the strain is building every day which will be released at some point soon causing a massive temblor.

According to Bilham, one region where the stress has not been relieved for the last almost 600 years is the Himalayan fault almost north of Delhi, the last big earthquake to have been recorded from this hot spot was way back in 1505. Extrapolating based on past fatalities caused due to historical earthquakes like the 8-magnitude earthquake that struck Kangra in 1905 and then factoring in for on the increased population densities, Bilham estimates '200,000 predictable fatalities', if a big one strikes now.

The World Bank has recently embarked on a month long 10,000-kilometres road journey along India's coast called 'Road to Resilience', which will end in Bhuj, the city that was devastated by a 7.7-magnitude earthquake 15 years ago on the morning of the Republic Day in 2001 which killed over 12,000 people. Saurabh Dani, senior disaster management specialist at The World Bank, Washington DC, USA says "India can do a lot more towards reducing the risk due to earthquakes".

The 'big one' is really waiting to happen just that we don't know where and when. Experts say the only way to diffuse the time bomb is to build safe. "So the message is that, if the past is the key to the present, a real big one is expected in the central Himalaya segment. Therefore get prepared", warns Rajendran. The old learning holds true "earthquakes don't kill it is really unsafe buildings that kill".

January 24, 2016

□

7

India: A Leader in Tsunami Warnings

Tsunami became a household word in India just about a decade ago when a devastating tsunami killed ten thousand people in a few minutes in southern India and overall some 230,000 people lost their lives in December 26, 2004 Indian Ocean tsunami.

Before that fateful Sunday morning, twelve years ago Indians literally did not know whether a tsunami is spelt with a 't' or 'p'. There was literally no memory of a tsunami having been experienced by the current generation in India. Since then there is huge recognition that tsunamis can be one of the most destructive natural forces on Earth. Lessons were learnt very quickly and today India is leader in the Indian Ocean region providing a 24×7 all year round tsunami early warning service from its high-tech facility in Hyderabad. Occasional vandalism by occupants of fishing boats that venture close to the sensors placed deep in the ocean makes system vulnerable to breakdown. These fisher folk steal the electronic parts and solar panels.

It is interesting to note that the Indian system has in its decade long existence has never ever issued a 'false warning', in contrast the much older and well-oiled Pacific Tsunami Warning Center regularly issues warnings that don't pan into real tsunamis eroding the credibility of the system. Sometimes late starters like India can quickly learn life-saving lessons that help forecasting in a big way.

An assessment by the United Nations Office for Disaster Risk Reduction (UNISDR) suggests that "tsunamis are rare. But they can be extremely deadly. In the past 100 years, more than 260,000 people have perished in 58 separate tsunamis. At an average of 4,600 deaths per disaster, the toll has surpassed any other natural hazard. Tsunamis know no borders, making international cooperation key for deeper political and public understanding of risk reduction measures."

This week the first world tsunami awareness day will be celebrated on November 5, 2016 spearheaded by the Indian Government. To commemorate the occasion, an event will be organised with at the Asian Ministerial Conference for Disaster Risk Reduction 2016, being held in New Delhi in collaboration with the United Nations Office for Disaster Risk Reduction (UNISDR).

According to UNISDR, the significance of this day, the 5th November, to tsunami awareness can be traced back to the year 1854. A villager in Wakayama Prefecture, Japan, was concerned about an impending tsunami after a high-intensity earthquake on November 5, 1854. He set up a fire to rice sheaves on the top of a hill. Fellow villagers, who went atop to put off the fire, were saved even as a tsunami destroyed their village down below. This was the first documented instance of a tsunami early warning. To commemorate that day of "Inamura no Hi" (the burning of rice sheaves), disaster experts spread awareness on tsunamis.

Tsunami are also called 'harbour waves', since they cause maximum damage in coastal areas and in harbours. Usual waves in the ocean and lakes are generated because of the gravitational pull of the moon and due to winds and these are usually very docile. But a tsunami is a wave which packs in a massive punch and can devastate coastal zones. Tsunamis travel across oceans at the speed at which and aeroplane flies and can circle the globe several times before they die off. In fact, ships plying in deep waters barely feel a tsunami passing underneath them but when the tsunami wave enters shallow regions the energy gets concentrated and can create waves as high as 20-30 metres and can travel several kilometres inland. At Nagapatinam and Cuddalore in Tamil Nadu after the 2004 tsunami, big boats could be seen left stranded several kilometres from the sea as the waves simply lifted them and deposited them way inland.

A tsunami can be generated when a massive underwater earthquake causes rapid displacement of water. The 2004 tsunami was generated because of a giant 9.1-magnitude earthquake off the west coast of Sumatra. Tsunamis can also be caused by underwater volcanic eruptions and landslips that happen below water among a few other reasons.

The entire Indian coastline of some 7500 kilometres is mostly vulnerable to be impacted by some tsunami or the other. The two main tsunami-genic regions closest for India are the massive earthquake fault zone that runs north to south in the Andaman and Nicobar Islands and the Makran Fault a region located south of Karachi city. Both these earthquake-prone zones can give rise to earthquakes that can generate devastating tsunamis.

Very soon after the 2004 tsunami India decided to set up a tsunami early warning system but it took almost three years for it to become fully operational. Made at a cost of about $ 20 million, it was remarkable that the Indian system was made with no cost or time overruns, in fact it was done well within the estimated budget. Today this system is manned all day and night by a dedicated staff of about a dozen people who ensure that timely warnings are issued.

According to Dr. Jitendra Singh, Minister of State in the Prime Minister's Office, the Indian Tsunami Early

Warning Centre (ITEWC) was established and made fully functional since 2007 and is now rendering operational services as a Regional Tsunami Watch Provider (RTWP) for whole of the Indian Ocean Region by the Indian National Centre for Ocean Information Sciences (INCOIS) located in Hyderabad. ITEWC comprises real-time seismic monitoring network broadband seismic stations apart from national and international seismic stations to detect undersea tsunami—genic earthquakes from the two known subduction zones of the Andaman-Sumatra and the Makran coast in the Indian Ocean which can potentially affect the Indian coastal states and island regions, a network of seven real-time sea-level sensors or tsunami buoys with bottom pressure recorders (BPR) in the open ocean, high frequency radars for coastal currents and 31 coastal tide gauge stations to capture tsunami wave amplitude on 24×7 basis. The data is analysed on a continuous basis. A host of communication systems are being employed for timely dissemination of advisories. India effectively utilizes its large fleet of satellites not only to gather data to predict a tsunami but also to disseminate the warnings.

The centre is capable of detecting tsunami-genic earthquakes occurring in the Indian Ocean Region as well as in the global oceans within 10 minutes of their occurrence and disseminated the advisories to the concerned authorities within 20 minutes through various modes of communication.

The Indian system works round the clock and in over a decade of my actively reporting about earthquakes and tsunamis the INCOIS system has almost never failed to answer questions be it middle of the night or day. The remarkable fact that the Hyderabad-based system has never issued a false warning is very creditable and that is because the scientists there will not issue an alert unless the sensors located deep inside the sea actually sense a change in pressure. Since the Indian system operationally caters only to the Indian nation the, INCOIS scientists are not under any fear of being sued. Unlike the Pacific system that caters to many nations and the workers manning that system have to always protect their backs against lawsuits. In India, the public knows that if a tsunami warning has been issued, it has to be taken really seriously. India does help out the Indian Ocean countries by only issuing advisories to the nodal points in the neighbouring countries who are then free to take necessary action on the ground.

Preparedness saves lives and India, along with 23 other Indian Ocean countries, recently participated in a tsunami mock drill on September 7-8, 2016. According to INCOIS in this first of its kind exercise around 40,000 people which is massive number were evacuated to safes places from around 350 coastal villages of 33 districts in coastal India. Interestingly, India's nuclear energy establishment that has many facilities on coastal India did not participate in the mock drill confirmed officials of INCOIS. It may be recalled that the massive destruction seen in the atomic power plants at Fukushima in Japan in 2011 was a consequence of a lack of preparedness to handle a giant tsunami. Though it must be said all nuclear power plants in India are installed with sensors that automatically shut down the rectors if a big earthquake hits them.

Since the inception of the tsunami early warning system in India, the country has been fortunate that not a single massive tsunami has hit the Indian coast, the real test comes in providing targeted forecasts that can accurately predict the arrival time and wave height. Last mile connectivity remains a hurdle. Evacuating people from the zone that may face the disaster is another Herculean task since convincing people to leave their homes and belongings is one of the toughest things. People are reluctant to vacate their homes when cyclones and hurricanes strike but at the same time effective, credible and timely communication in local languages helps people feel confident to takc shelter. Trust has to be won as enforced evacuations don't work that well.

Preparedness holds the key and it is well-known that natural hazards turn disasters when effective communication fails. Community preparedness can save maximum lives when they are ably assisted by high-tech facilities like the Indian tsunami early warning system.

October 30, 2016

□

8

Science gets a tight embrace in the Modi government

Is the glass of science half full or half empty by way of support for S&T-related activities in the first two years of the Prime Minister Narendra Modi government? Half full would be a more appropriate phrase but holes due to a lack of legislative business are draining the gains that could have actually accrued faster.

There can now be no doubts that the Modi-led government, which completed two years in office, believes in the intrinsic value of supporting Indian science and technology. Being a right leaning government, there were many apprehensions that the National Democratic Alliance (NDA) government would put road-blocks for the development of modern science with its leaders probably harping more on old Hindu philosophy and glories of India as a powerhouse in ancient Vedic times. While some of that did take place but by-and-large the focus has remained on how to mainstream the benefits accruing from indigenous innovation to the common person.

Early in his term, almost within a month, Modi himself set the tone when he was sighted at the Indian space port to witness the launch of a rocket and then he gave a stirring speech from there on June 30, 2014 on the launch of the Polar Satellite Launch Vehicle, where he called the Indian scientific community 'brilliant'. This was the first time the erstwhile 'chaiwallah' Modi used a tele-prompter in the public as Prime Minister and showed that he could woo India using modern technology. In quick succession, he also embraced and engaged with the nuclear scientists and the agriculture community. That the government withstood two back-to-back failed monsoons and did not let the spirits of the Indian public flag show that 'policy paralysis' was a thing of the past.

To Modi's credit, he has appointed as ministers for science politicians who have a deep understanding of the sector. The first science minister was Dr. Jitendra Singh, a specialist on diabetes who has published several books on medical science. In a reshuffle in November 2014, Dr. Harsh Vardhan was brought in as cabinet minister for science, a soft-spoken, well-meaning politician, who connects easily with the mercurial Indian scientists. A junior minister in Y. S. Chowdary, an industrialist-turned-politician was also sworn in. Since then, Dr. Vardhan whose first love is undoubtedly health and a man better known for 'eradicating polio from India' has relentlessly toured many laboratories to pump up the morale of the scientists. To take stock of the living conditions of scientists, Dr. Vardhan even spent a night on India's research ship Sindhu Sadhana, cruising the depths of the Arabian Sea. A man of deep convictions, Dr. Vardhan is probably the only minister who says 'he prayed that a scientific forecast by his own ministry would go wrong'. This was after the India Meteorological Department had predicted a drought in 2015. Gods did not favour him then, but hopefully his prayers that 2016 be a good monsoon year come true.

Modi has earned the wrath of high-ranking Indian boffins since much to the annoyance of many top Indian scientists. Modi has all but abandoned the high-profile Science Advisory Council to the Prime Minister (SAC-

PM). Even though the outgoing chairman of the SAC-PM, Professor C.N.R. Rao had openly endorsed Modi by saying, 'He is definitely a man with vision. There is no question that he wants to do something. We hope he will not only use good advice and all the wonderful ideas he has. He is obviously a doer when you listen to him; there is nothing wrong in what he says. What Modi says is perfect.' A rare endorsement from a scientist who has had a long-long innings with the Congress-led governments.

It is not as if all has been hunky-dory under the Modi-Vardhan combination. There are several important S&T-related legislations that are lying in cold storage that need to be passed soon. The National Biotech Regulatory Authority Bill has been pending for a long-long time and there is no sign of it seeing the light of day. As a consequence, application of biotechnology is suffering since the government is unwilling to take a decision on releasing more genetically modified varieties of crops into the farmer's fields. Dr. Vardhan also needs to clarify once and for all if he wants the Indian biotech industry to grow by $ 20 billion a year or by $ 10 billion. Similarly, the Human DNA Profiling Bill seems to have been still born.

On the money front, scientists in India were preparing for the worst – a drastic cut in the budgetary allocations. However, the Finance Minister Arun Jaitley surprised them in 2016 by being benevolent and has given the Ministry of Science and Technology a ₹ 811 crore increase in the central plan outlay as compared to the last fiscal, which represents an upswing of about 11%. The Department of Biotechnology (DBT) came out getting a ₹ 193 crore increase, which represented a 12% increase over the last fiscal.

The Department of Scientific and Industrial Research, which also accommodates the massive Council of Scientific and Industrial Research (CSIR) having a network of 37 labs, came worst off with an almost flat budget. Even then, there was also reason for some huge relief since in 2015, at a meeting in Dehradun of all directors of CSIR, Vardhan had pushed through a proposal that 'all CSIR labs to make efforts to be self-financing in the next 2 years'. This had sent shock waves among the 16,000 staff who felt that CSIR would soon become a low-cost contract research organisation and the lofty goals of doing 'blue sky research' could be given a 'go by'.

Yet scientists like Syed Hasnain, a biotechnologist at the Indian Institute of Technology, Delhi, are not chuffed, who says 'high profile medical research facilities like the Indian Council of Medical Research (ICMR) have declared a research holiday since no funds are available'. In contrast, health minister J. P. Nadda says there is no shortage of funds for the health sector but it is a lack of timely utilisation that bothers him.

No doubt that Modi is a space buff and it was at Sriharikota on June 30, 2014 that Modi mandated India Space Research Organisation (ISRO) to make a 'SAARC Satellite' for use by our neighbours as a gift from India – a proposition that even took the then leadership of ISRO by complete surprise. Modi's good intentions were put paid as in less than two years, the satellite was renamed South Asia Satellite as Pakistan refused to back this initiative. Even though ISRO forges ahead and hopes to launch the friendly communications satellite by the end of this year. Meanwhile, at less than ₹ 1500 crores and using just seven satellites in orbit, ISRO has given India the satellite-based navigation system or Navigation with Indian Constellation (NAVIC). Most recently, a few days before the second birthday of the Modi government, ISRO stunned the world by successfully launching a 'swadeshi space shuttle', a technology that promises to lower launch costs by ten times.

In less than 60 days of assuming office as Prime Minister, on July 21, 2014, Modi himself flew into India's main nuclear facility, the Bhabha Atomic Research Centre (BARC) in Mumbai to take stock of the country's nuclear capabilities. Usually, PMs are quietly briefed about India's prowess in this area but to make sure the world knows that he has his fingers firmly on India's nuclear trigger, Modi spent a whole afternoon inside the BARC. Modi expressed his 'strong appreciation for the extraordinary achievements of Indian scientific community'. Despite this unique visit, the Nuclear Safety Regulatory Authority bill has not been taken up by the government with the right earnest, even though other amendments that needed to be made for commercial use of nuclear energy have sailed through the Parliament. Modi has also not been able to ink any deal to buy and install any foreign atomic reactors in India.

At the same time, the high profile 'Make in India' program has left many scientists confused on what then happens to the 'Made in India' towards that the science ministry needs to upgrade its science, technology and innovation policy, which remains a work in progress. Experts have said that unless Indian scientists discover and innovate in India, 'Make in India' would remain a mere slogan. Buck up Mr. Modi, your time is fast running out; the honeymoon period is over; and the Indian public seeks deliverables. Well begun is half done. Today there are more hits than misses by the Modi government in its support towards science in India.

May 28, 2016

□

ENERGY

9

Is Solar Power the Real Solution to India's Energy Crisis?

India unfolded a much-hyped 'Solar Alliance', on the side lines of the climate change conference in Paris. A grand invitation extended to the 121 sunny nations to come together for making solar power accessible, its headquarters in Gurgaon and the Indian Government seeks to inject ₹ 400 crores as seed money.

Now an impression has been created that solar power could be the panacea for solving all issues related to climate change and energy independence for India. This is far from the truth. Since despite the aggressive international marketing even for India during the next 4-5 decades 'coal will still be the king'! Today about sixty per cent of India's power is generated using hydrocarbons.

There is no doubt that India loves the Sun God and the country as a whole is bestowed with more than 300 sunny days which makes it a very attractive option to generate electricity. However, there is still a huge catch the Sun is available only for half a day and hence excessive over-reliance on solar power can be very hazardous during darkness.

Today the country plans to ramp up its solar power generating capacity to 100,000 MW by 2022, an almost twenty-five-fold increase from 4000 MW of installed capacity in 2015. This means every year India will have to install about 14,000 MW of solar power continuously for the next seven years if this ambitious 100 gigawatt target has to be achieved. What is the past record of accomplishment, in the last five years India put up only about 2000 MW of installed solar power.

Several bottlenecks still need to be overcome in harnessing solar power for generating electricity. Today even the best of the best commercially available solar photo voltaic cells give and efficiency less than 20% which is a relatively poor conversion ratio and it is for this reason that solar cells have to have large surface areas. This when translated means very large tracts of land area would get covered with solar panels if the equivalent of 100,000 MW has to be generated.

The other and bigger bottleneck is the need for storage of generated power. Since solar panels are no good when there is no sunlight like say at night or during the heavy clouds that cover the sky during the monsoons, in these non-sunny hours the generated electricity needs to be stored in batteries, which can then supply power. Today's batteries are really very expensive, and life span is relatively short and trying to deploy them on Giga watt capacities is no joke. For solar power to make a big inroad, a huge breakthrough needs to be made in battery technology. There used to be a promise of plastic batteries that kind of fizzled out last century. Hopefully, this new 'Breakthrough Energy Coalition', announced by Microsoft founder Bill Gates along with 28 super rich investors could spur research and development in making cheap, durable, light weight and long-lasting re-chargeable batteries. Until then the reliance on good old Lead Acid batteries will be the mainstay for industrial scale applications.

Assuming that efficiencies of solar cells and batteries are kind of resolved with great investments in research the literally unresolvable issue that solar power is an intermittent source is never going to fade away, available during daylight and off during night this makes it intermittent. There is certain baseload of power that is always required whether it is day or night and that will always have to be met with non-renewable energy sources.

This basepower is that load which is required to be available one hundred per cent of the times irrespective of whether the Sun is shining or not, the wind is blowing or not. As of today, there are only two reliable sources of meeting the baseloads, good old coal and gas both of which give out that climate villain called carbon dioxide and the other gorilla called atomic energy. If one analyses carefully the details of India's submissions as part of the Intended National Determined Contributions (INDCs) the Indian energy pie envisages a mix of not more than forty per cent for renewable energy by 2030. Some experts even suggest that having a huge mix of intermittent renewable energy in the grid could actually lead to its collapse.

When translated this essentially means that bulk of India's energy will be generated using hydrocarbon and nuclear. A healthy energy mix is pre-requisite for long-term energy independence.

Much is also being made out that a foreign vendor bid to supply solar power at ₹ 4.63 a unit for a solar park in Andhra Pradesh by Sun Edison Inc. a US-based company. This was part of transparent e-auction asserts the Union Energy Minister Piyush Goyal which aggressively brought the prices down almost comparable to thermal power. However, one will have to wait and watch to see if at such low prices these projects really take off and get completed. Sources in the Bureau of Energy Efficiency say enough safeguards have been put in place to ensure defaulters do not go scot-free. But in the past if one recalls aggressive bidding hiked the prices of 3G spectrum beyond expectation and since then private companies have been having a tough time unrolling the services to the fullest and the omnipresent call drops are symptomatic of that malaise. On similar lines, there are fears that solar companies who have bid at such aggressively low per unit rates may default when actual solar parks have to come up.

There is no doubt that the climate is changing but to make out that nations as large as India which may have a population of 1.5 billion in a few decades could be run only on solar power seems far-fetched, unless of course breakthrough takes place in battery technology. Here there is no doubt India is not investing enough. A judicious mix of several forms of energy is the ideal solution.

December 6, 2015

□

ENVIRONMENT

10

Everyday Plastics Spell Doom for the Oceans

The ubiquitous plastic easy to use and easy to discard and forms part of our everyday lives is unwittingly spelling a doom for the oceans and its myriads of creatures.

It is not only the littering by water bottles, wrappers, bags, nets and industrial waste that is causing havoc, but the smaller broken down components of these plastic components called 'microplastics', that are becoming a new and hidden menace.

Dr. S.W.A Naqvi, "Director of the National Institute of Oceanography, Goa says 'plastic pollution, is very big problem and pollution of the global oceans with micro-plastics is only now being estimated in times to come it will become a huge problem that will dog humanity for centuries since plastics outlive humans by a factor of ten."

Fishes, whales, seals and turtles mistakenly eat the larger objects like plastic bags and bottles and these objects then choke their guts. The degraded pieces of larger plastic refuse also pose a problem as they are ingested in smaller biota and from where they enter the food web often finally ending as part of food for humans.

Striking an alarming note on the pollution caused by plastics, Dr. Mahua Saha, a scientist who works on marine pollution at the National Institute of Oceanography (NIO) in Goa, reports that the world population now produces close to its own weight in plastics every year.

A 2015 global study published in reputed American journal *Science* estimated that 275 million metric tons of plastic waste was generated worldwide in 192 coastal countries with as much as 12.7 million metric tons entered the oceans as waste.

A 2015 report from the World Watch Institute, Washington DC finds that "approximately 10-20 million tons of plastic end up in the oceans each year. A recent study conservatively estimated that 5.25 trillion plastic particles weighing a total of 268,940 tons are currently floating in the world's oceans. This plastic debris results in an estimated $13 billion a year in losses from damage to marine ecosystems".

Every year each Indian uses about eight kilograms of plastic according to an estimate by the Central Pollution Control Board (CPCB) meaning annually India consumes a whopping eight million metric tons of plastic. A 2013 study by CPCB revealed that about 15,340 tons per day of plastic waste was generated every day and carrybags made of low-density polyethylene make a bulk of the waste.

The 2015 study from the University of Georgia, USA ranked India twelfth in the list of countries that mismanaged its plastic waste and let it contaminate the oceans. Leading the pack is China followed by Indonesia, Philippines, Vietnam and Sri Lanka. It estimated that 340 grams of plastic waste is generated in India per person per day with China topping the list almost three times more waste being generated. The study suggests that in coastal areas of India about 87% of the plastic waste is mismanaged.

Saha says "plastics are really a very big threat to humans", who adds that more than 80% of all marine debris originates from the land and according to her some plastic bags can take up to a 1000 years to degrade, and even when they degrade they continue to pose a huge risk to living organisms.

Plastics pose a double whammy, to make some of them flexible often toxic compounds are mixed as additives and some of these as they bioaccumulate can be cancer causing. In addition, Saha points out that since plastics are essentially organic solids they over time as they float around they absorb toxic chemicals and when these in turn are gobbled by the living organisms the toxic chemicals tend to start accumulating in the fat tissues and can lead to growth of tumours and cancers.

To get a better understanding on the magnitude of the problem that India's over 7500 kilometre long coastline faces due to pollution by plastics, the NIO is all set to launch a ₹ 90 lakh three year project to map the magnitude of the problem. Every beach in Goa is contaminated with plastics exclaims Saha. A 2006 study found that in the ship-breaking yard of Alang in Gujarat every ten kilograms of sediment contained about one gram of plastic waste no trivial amount since actually there should be none.

On a recent cruise on India's research ship to her surprise Saha found plastic debris even at 700-800 meter depth below the sea. Saha exclaims the scourge of plastics is contaminating the deep seas as well. In the deep seas, the microplastic particles often smaller than the human hair enter the plankton or the main food producers of the oceans, then a vicious cycle begins as they find their way through the complex food chains into the edible fishes and often end up on our food plates.

Interestingly, Saha reports that India has the highest rates of plastic recycling topping at 47% which means that still more than half of the plastics India consumes ends as waste.

'Reduce, reuse, recycle, rebuy and re-think', should be the governing principle when plastics are used says Saha who terms 'saying no to plastics', is the easiest solution to eliminating the long-term threat that plastic pollution poses to survival of life in the oceans. Hence, a 'Swach Bharat' is good for the survival of all life forms.

October 4, 2015

□

11

Beef Eating is Bad for Environment. Shun Beef Save the Planet say Experts!

Beef eating has impassioned the nation, with politicians of all hues duelling like bulls in rage. Religious taboos are one aspect but there is also a very strong environmental angle for not eating beef. The United Nations Environment Program (UNEP) has dubbed beef as a 'climate harmful meat'. It is very energy intensive to produce every gram of beef on an average every hamburger results in three kilograms of carbon emissions to the atmosphere. Today, saving the planet is really about ensuring sustainable consumption and meat production is unfortunately a highly energy-intensive exercise.

Meat eaters in general and beef eaters in particular are among the most unfriendly to the global environment reports the United Nations body the Food and Agriculture Organisation (FAO) in Rome. It may come as a surprise but globally beef production is one of the leading culprits for climate change. Some even suggest that beef is the devil or the *'shaitan'* of the meat production industry. That said the lynching of man on the suspicion that he consumed beef can never be justified in any society.

Experts suggest that giving up beef will reduce the global carbon footprint on Earth far more than avoiding use of cars! Here is why, if one examines the numbers closely livestock production contributes more towards global warming than does the transport sector in total, through emissions of gases that result in changing the climate. According to FAO, the livestock sector is responsible for 18% of the global greenhouse gas emissions as compared the transport sectors 15%. In a study "Livestock's Long Shadow: Environmental Issues and Options" the FAO concludes that "the livestock sector is major player [and its contributions to climate change has] a higher share than transport".

Earth lovers are voicing their concern and shaming meat eaters, most recently Laurence Tubiana the charismatic French Ambassador for Climate Change Negotiations for the big climate summit to be held in a few weeks in Paris said "this overconsumption of meat is really killing many things [there has to be a campaign] that big meat consumers should stop that. At least try one day without meat."

According to a 2012 estimate by Ministry of Agriculture, India is home to 512 million livestock of which cows and buffaloes together account for 111 million animals. Most of the animals in India are not reared for slaughtering, but prized for milk and ploughing. UNEP estimates that in 2012 the world was home to 1.43 billion cattle.

So do not start feeling guilty that Indians are highly environment-friendly when measured on the scale of meat eating and livestock numbers. A landmark 2012 study "Growing Greenhouse Gas Emissions due to Meat Production", by UNEP finds that on an average Indians consume only 12 grams of meat per person per day which is almost ten times lower than the global average of 115 grams. In comparison, USA leads with over 322 grams of meat being eaten per person per day with China at about 160. Hence, on an average a meat-eating American contributes 25 times more to global warming as compared to a non-vegetarian Indian.

A 2012 estimate by the Department of Animal Husbandry, Dairying and Fisheries says the country produced 5.9 million tonnes of meat of which poultry's (mostly chicken) contribution to the total meat production is about half with less than 5% of the meat coming from beef. In comparison in 2009, the world produced 278 million tonnes of meat, which means that India accounts for just about 2% of the world's meat production while housing 17% of the world's population. There is no doubt that meats provide the vital protein and nutrients needed for proper human development. Milk is a healthy substitute.

It may sound astounding but beef production on an average requires 28 times more land and causes 11 times more global warming as compared to other livestock categories found a 2014 study by the prestigious Yale University in USA, published in the *Proceedings of the National Academy of Sciences* which concluded that "minimizing beef consumption mitigates the environmental costs of diet most effectively". Tim Benton of the University of Leeds, UK, not associated with US study felt "the biggest intervention people could make towards reducing their carbon footprints would not be to abandon cars, but to eat significantly less red meat".

Beef production is also bad for water conservation, since cattle rearing for beef require almost ten times more water as compared to staple crops like wheat and rice. In contrast, pork production uses three times less water as compared to beef ranching. Cattle also emit a highly potent climate changing gas called 'methane' in their farts and through belching. Also called 'marsh gas' this inflammable gas is produced in the guts of cattle by the bacteria as they digest the food of ruminants and methane is 21 times more potent than carbon dioxide in causing global warming.

Using data from a Swedish study, the UNEP says "in terms of greenhouse gas emissions the consumption of

1 kg domestic beef in a household represents automobile use of a distance of 160 kilometres". This means a car travelling all the way from New Delhi to Agra would cause about the same amount of global climate change as is done by consuming just one kilogram of beef! No wonder beef is considered highly environmentally un-friendly. Nevertheless, at the same time in dry and arid regions of the world livestock are considered a 'savings bank' by local people as they form part of the life-saving kit to overcome the harsh environment.

Meat eating may not be 'green' but as more and more people become affluent, meat is becoming chic and fashionable. FAO estimates that by 2050 the global meat consumption will rise to 460 million tonnes. The global environment watchdog the UNEP recommends a shift to 'less climate harmful' meats and emphasizes that "healthy eating is not just important for the individual but for the planet as whole".

October 11, 2015

□

12

In a Global First, the World Bank goes to a Zoo in India!

The World Bank usually tames wild economies and helps countries stabilize their fluctuating finances, but in a global first, the banker for the world has gone to a zoo that too in India! This is a new addition in the portfolio of the bank as part of its ever-expanding work on urban regeneration.

A zoo is nothing but a bank of captive animals. In a novel initiative, The World Bank has embraced a zoo for its eco-development! In Visakhapatnam, the global bank is extending an assistance of $20 million to help reconstruct the Indira Gandhi Zoological Park (IGZP), which got devastated during cyclone Hudhud. This is part of the $370 million Andhra Pradesh Disaster Recovery Project for which the bank is extending assistance of $250 million from 2015-20.

The much-loved Vizag Zoo is nestled in the picturesque Eastern Ghats. It sees an annual footfall of about eight lakh people and was set up in 1972 and shot into fame because it had some aviaries designed by the legendary ornithologist Dr. Salim Ali the 'Bird Man of India'.

Dr. Neha Vyas, senior environment specialist at the India country office of The World Bank who is actively involved in this eco-development project asserts that this is "the very first time in the history of The World Bank that it is directly involved in a zoo".

The Vizag Zoo situated on the northern limit of the Visakhapatnam town houses 170 different species of animals on its 250-hectare campus. Only a road separates the zoo from the sea and this became its undoing, when cyclone Hudhud struck the region it caused huge damage to the entire Zoo. According to a damages needs assessment report by The World Bank almost 40% of the trees of the complex were flattened and a larger number were damaged. Some 180 birds and animals escaped from their enclosures as the cages were badly damaged and 11 animals died due to the cyclone. Out of 67 enclosures about 57 suffered damages. "Unfortunately for the Zoo the eye of the cyclone Hudhud passed right over it causing widespread devastation in the Zoological Park", says Vyas. The enclosures for tiger, python and the white tiger were severely damaged. The offices including the veterinary hospital were also affected and the compound wall was breached in several places. The adjoining Kambalakonda Wildlife Sanctuary was also damaged.

Cyclone Hudhud was classed in the 'very severe' category and it crashed into Andhra Pradesh on October 12, 2014. Sixty-one people lost their lives in the natural calamity. According to the Andhra Pradesh Government, cyclone Hudhud affected about 9.2 million people in over 7,285 villages in four coastal districts of the state. The damage caused by the cyclone was due to the unprecedented wind velocity of over 200 kilometer per hour followed by torrential rains that caused massive destruction in the districts of Visakhapatnam, Srikakulam, Vizianagaram and East Godavari. According to The World Bank, the cyclone caused a damage equivalent of $2155 million and over two lakh houses were affected.

At the Zoological Park where local support to retain it on its original location is widespread, The World Bank partnering with the AP Forest Department and the Central Zoo Authority will help bring back the pristine glory of the Zoo. It will also help re-build the eco-tourism park at the Kambalakonda Wildlife Sanctuary. At the Zoo the effort will be to build in disaster resilience into the civil structures; re-establish lost nurseries to establish green shelter beds that act as windbreaks. Deepak Singh, senior disaster management expert at The World Bank's India office says "the endeavour is to demonstrate how a disaster resilient zoo can be scientifically re-modelled". Who adds that "the zoo plays an important part in the education, recreation and conservation and it fits in nicely in the concept of having a 'smart Visakhapatnam"'.

The World Bank has a portfolio of about $26 billion for India where it partners in about 89 projects. Disaster management and recovery is becoming a big part of The World Bank's activities in India where it is providing assistance of about $2.2 billion for 10 projects.

In a one of its kind rolling audit on wheels to assess the impact of its efforts on the coastal projects, a ten member multinational team of The World Bank is currently visiting all ten coastal states on a specially designed bus that will tour the Indian coast for a month.

Called 'Road to Resilience', the 10,000 kilometre continuous road trip on this special bus by the officials of The World Bank will travel all along the Indian coast from West Bengal to Gujarat and will provide support and oversight for the six coastal projects. The team reaches the Visakhapatnam and will visit the Zoo later this week after having visited the Sunderbans and the cyclone-prone areas of Odisha where The World Bank is helping set up over 300 multi-purpose cyclone relief shelters.

Vyas says at the Visakhapatnam Zoo "effort is to ensure ecological restoration of an area that will be resilient and have a minimum footprint", for a large outdoor recreational area almost within the city limits. The World Bank is currently in talks with the Smithsonian Institution that runs the world famous National Zoo in Washington DC, USA to see if their expertise can be tapped to re-develop the Vizag Zoo as a model 21st century *'Ecological Park'*. The IGZP is already a breeding centre for the Indian Wild Dog or the Dhole and it is hoped the 'modern', version will house an even better breeding centre.

Restoration of the IGZP is a pet project of the Mr. N. Chandrababu Naidu, the Chief Minister of Andhra Pradesh who has vowed to make it even better than the Nehru Zoological Park at Hyderabad in Telangana and the current effort is likely to offer a working blueprint for setting up a state-of-the-art Zoo at Guntur the upcoming capital of Andhra Pradesh.

This unique one of its kind push by The World Bank where it is providing assistance to an Indian zoo will add value to the 100 'Smart City' initiative being spearheaded by Prime Minister Narendra Modi where urban regeneration and open spaces are key elements.

January 17, 2016

□

13

New Delhi Choking! Root Cause Stems from a Deep Crisis in Indian Agriculture!

North India faces an annual trauma as winter approaches the air in the region that houses more than 200 million people becomes toxic. Fingers are pointed at the hand that feeds India, farmers in the granary of the country are rebuked asking them not to burn agriculture waste in their fields as their action fouls the air in mega cities like New Delhi, Lucknow and Allahabad.

There is no doubt that after the monsoon ends the vast paddy fields in India's granary Haryana and Punjab turn into cremation grounds where the leftover paddy straw is burnt in vast swathes. The fires are so many and so widespread that satellites flying hundreds of kilometres above the Earth record their presence. Giving *'Udta Punjab'* a whole new dirty air dimension. This is also the time when generally the westerly winds prevail and a giant plume of smoke covers north India. Satellite pictures depict the smoke plume with clarity and alarm bells starting ringing in the corridors of power in India's capital.

Last winter even the Supreme Court Chief Justice of India passed strict orders and even contributed his ritual bit by car-pooling, despite his efforts the air remains toxic. Delhi's air is a complex cocktail of noxious exhausts from automobiles, industry, thermal power plants and 'charvested' or burnt fields. Nobody really knows who is the bigger culprit.

But it is easy to point fingers at the farmers little realizing that behind the farmers burning agricultural waste is deep-deep crisis that is brewing in agriculture and it is hugely interlinked to all the elementary ingredients for a healthy life, air, water and land.

Today the fields of Haryana and Punjab are being tormented so much so that they are losing productivity, the haloed Green Revolution is turning them into debt-ridden wastelands.

Long years ago, the region used to harvest one or two crops a year and in-between fields were left fallow. This fallow period was very crucial as it gave the organic matter from agricultural waste time to decompose and mix with the top soil. Today in most places at least three crops are being farmed if not four. As soon as one crop is harvested, the farmers are eager to start planting the next crop. There is no time to let the paddy waste, to be used more judiciously, in the rush to drive ahead with the next crop the simplest alternative for farmers is to burn the waste, and to let the ash sink into the soil. This gives agriculture a whole new definition, 'slash and burn farming green revolution style' or what I call '*jhuming* Punjab style'.

A vicious cycle is brewing, farmers have been lured into cultivating more and more from their fields mainly because of faulty agriculture policies followed for many decades. As the Indian agri-researchers gave the country more and more short duration varieties farmers kept embracing them with gay abandon, nobody even gave a thought what it was doing to the soil health and now leading to unprecedented air pollution.

If one travels through Punjab and Haryana in May and June which is the peak of summer and temperatures are sizzling hovering around the 45 degrees centigrade mark, it is traumatic to see fields being flooded with water pumped from deep inside mother Earth and paddy sowing being done. With the monsoon at least 6-8 weeks away farmers made greedy by state subsidies start paddy cultivation in Sahara Desert like weather conditions. Paddy is crop that thrives at times when water is plenty so artificially water is made available to flood the fields.

This early sowing of paddy leads to a double whammy, initially ground water is pumped up using copious amounts of energy. This not only depletes the water table which is most places has been falling to unprecedented levels recently NASA using its satellites called it 'an unprecedented crisis of vanishing water'. Remarking that "if measures are not taken to ensure sustainable groundwater usage, consequences for the 114 million residents of the region may include a collapse of agricultural output and severe shortages of potable water," explained Matt Rodell, based at NASA's Goddard Space Flight Center in Greenbelt, USA. NASA reported that groundwater levels have been declining by an average of one meter every three years (one foot per year). More than 109 cubic km (26 cubic miles) of groundwater disappeared between 2002 and 2008—double the capacity of India's largest surface water reservoir. Who cares for sustainability!

The second big problem arises once the crop has been harvested which happens during the post-monsoon season, at that point the rice grains are sold at government determined minimum support prices and the farmers are left with a large amounts of straw. Unfortunately, straw from paddy contains a lot of silica and is very rough and hence bovines find it very difficult to eat it. Now when the farmers are in a hurry to plant the next crop, they are left with no alternative but to hurriedly burn the agri-waste.

Waiting to make organic compost out of the straw or

to roll it into bales and transport it to the few agri-waste to wealth power generators is both costly on time and money. So going in for *'jhum agriculture with a Punjabi tadka"* by incinerating the waste on location is a cheap and simple solution as it costs merely a match stick. Organic matter is the life blood of any top soil but in regions of north western India organic carbon content is constantly being depleted at a rapid rate, experts say very soon they will turn into wastelands.

According to a recent State of Environment of Punjab published by the local, government, "open field burning of straw after combine harvesting is a common practice in the state in order to ensure early preparation of fields for the next crop. Punjab produces around 23 million tons of rice straw and 17 million tons of wheat straw annually. More than 80% of paddy straw (18.4 million tons) and almost 50% wheat straw (8.5 million tons) produced in the state is being burnt in fields every year. Apart from affecting the soil fertility, this also causes air pollution due to emission of large amounts of suspended particulate matter besides gases like methane, carbon monooxide, oxides of nitrogen and sulphur dioxide among others leading to various health hazards like respiratory, skin and eye diseases. Intensive agriculture is also a contributor to greenhouse gases like, carbon dioxide, methane and nitrous oxide causing climate change."

To top it all the State of Environment of Punjab report points out that "declining farm yield and income due to economic (high cost of inputs like, seeds, fertilizers, pesticides and farm labour) and ecological (low productivity of soil, receding water table) factors is pushing marginal and small farmers into the vicious cycle of debt. The total indebtedness is around ₹ 240 million (50% each from institutional and non-institutional sources) for the loans taken for tractors, tubewells, farm chemicals, seeds, as well as, for other social needs. As per results of a recent survey, the indebtedness of Punjab farmers on an average is ₹ 41,576/- (against the national average of ₹ 12,585/-). Sixty-five point four per cent of farmer households are under debt in the state, next only to Andhra Pradesh (82%) and Tamil Nadu (74.5%)."

So when most farmers are custodians of innate native wisdom why are they indulging in such profligate and damaging practices, unfortunately it is really the government's agri-economic policies that are to blame. Subsidized or free electricity to farmers makes them use their pump-sets endlessly and then on top of it an assured minimum support price gives them a ready market, leaving no incentive to be considerate towards the top soil, deep acquirers and mother Earth in general and now this new headache of being dubbed the fountain head of widespread air pollution.

To solve this giant mess, knee-jerk reactions like Delhi Chief Minister Arvind Kejriwal's 'odd even scheme' to ration cars on the roads and passing dictates to farmers not to burn agri-waste and to penalize are just not going to work. A comprehensive restructuring of the agricultural economy is required if denizens of Delhi and north India don't want to choke to death. Nobody has the time to implement such mega changes so the National Green Tribunal (NGT) will keep passing more and more draconian but unimplementable orders and clean air which is really a fundamental right of every citizen will become more and more toxic by the day. A slow painful death is the only surety.

October 23, 2016

□

14

Killer Air: Solution to Pollution is not Dilution but Better Public Transportation

There is no doubt that the killer air is causing a slow poisoning of India's capital. Nevertheless, the quick-fix solution to pollution is not dilution. There is no doubt that New Delhi needs to reduce its air pollution, but to an analytical mind, the odds that the 'odd-even' vehicle rationing system unilaterally imposed by the Chief Minister of Delhi, Arvind Kejriwal may not bring about the desired results in quantitatively controlling air pollution.

At the turn of the century, when Compressed Natural Gas (CNG) was introduced on orders of the Supreme Court of India, the killer air over Delhi indeed cleared out, but then such a clinically radical measure is just not being attempted but a tame politically correct solution is being tried. Ideally, the only solution is to make public transportation cheap and convenient so that India's love affair with diesel-fired cars is curbed.

If one looks at the source apportionment study of air pollution put together by a civil engineer Mukesh Sharma from IIT, Kanpur, one finds that vehicles are not the biggest culprit for causing air pollution; but mostly road dust and construction dust are the devil. Two-thirds of the particulate matter below 10 microns or PM-10 can be attributed to dust and about 40% of the PM 2.5 is accounted by road dust. Vehicles at best contribute between 9% and 20% of the PM-10 and PM-2.5 levels respectively. So, vehicles are really not the worst polluters.

If one further analyses data from the IIT-Kanpur study, which itself still remains a 'draft report' and who knows how the data may change. Among the entire vehicular population of Delhi, the biggest polluters are trucks, contributing about half the pollution followed by two-wheelers that contribute two-thirds of the pollution. Four-wheelers contribute only a tenth of the pollution of Delhi.

To take the 'odd-even' rationing formula a bit further, at best, half of the four-wheelers will be off the roads between 8 am and 8 pm in the first half of January. This should theoretically reduce the pollution load caused by four-wheelers by half, but then, since they are not the biggest villains, to expect that the air would be cleaner really needs a quantum jump in imagination.

In addition, since 'car-pooling' is being recommended in a big way, it would not be 'odd to assume' that the 'odd' car that works on an 'odd' day would not be over-working as extra 'car-pooled' passengers will need to be dropped. This should incrementally increase the pollution load. In addition, one may see old, more polluting vehicles being plied on the roads since citizens need to even their lives on odd days. Experts also fear that people who can afford may actually buy more vehicles, so causing a spike in car numbers. Maybe the Delhi Government seeks to mop up more one-time lumpsum road tax collection revenues.

It is reported that the 'odd-even' formula for rationing vehicles on roads, whenever it is implemented to clean the dirty air over Paris, the city authorities in France attract the citizens to public transportation by making it free of charge. Maybe the next populist measure the Aam Admi Party Government of Delhi could implement is to make travel on the Delhi Metro and the Delhi Transport Corporation free for the days when road rationing is implemented.

As Sunita Narain from the Centre for Science and Environment, New Delhi points out that the National Capital Region (NCR) houses the country's worst polluting Badarpur Power Station that incidentally continues to operate and ironically the country's cleanest thermal power station located at Bawana in the NCR remains shut down, since there is shortfall of Piped Natural Gas.

A drop in a few percentage points of air pollution may actually not be noticeable at all if one were to factor in weather patterns since such small variations happen on a daily basis depending on whether there is strong surface wind that dilutes the pollution by sweeping it away into the hinterland. Dr. M. Rajeevan, an atmospheric scientist and Secretary of the Ministry of Earth Sciences, New Delhi, says not enough is known quantitatively on how air pollution dilutes in the atmosphere over Delhi since the contribution of weather and wind in dispersing toxic gasses in the chaos of the tropical atmosphere over Delhi remains a mysterious unknown X-factor.

The well-intentioned thrust to control air pollution by the Delhi Government may actually boomerang since the desired results of controlling air pollution may not be forthcoming since quick-fix solutions tend to break down easily. Moreover, if the citizens cooperate whole-heartedly with Kejriwal and they still do not witness a perceptible drop in pollution levels, they would be highly dejected. A flagging public support would augur very badly in the long-term effort at controlling the killer air that is poisoning our lungs.

Therefore, solution to pollution is not dilution but a long term well thought out strengthening of the already quaking public transport system of the National Capital Region.

December 31, 2015

□

HEALTH

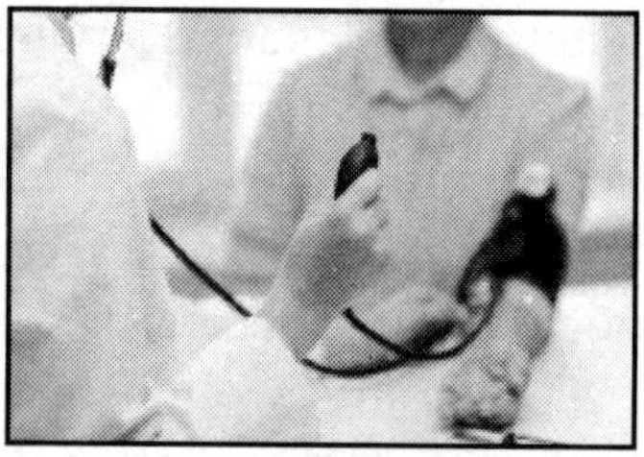

15

The Weight Loss Paradox: Low Fat Diets are No better than High Fat Diets in the Long-Term!

The festival of lights Diwali is over and the binging on sweets that comes with the much-loved festival would have made many think of losing some weight. Here is a reality on check what diets to subscribe too.

Dieting is hard to comply and only a very few lose weight from dieting on a long-term basis. Now a new study surprisingly indicates that sticking to 'low fat diets' has little consequence on long-term weight loss. 'Low fat' labels advertised on foods attract many gullible consumers. New studies may just force the huge 'low fat healthy foods' industry to go in for a re-think, or at least the consumers can question them.

For any weight, loss program what matters most is that more calories are burnt than what are consumed and towards this exercising regularly is the best option with restrained intake of food.

Analysing this long-term study, the leading British journal *Nature* concluded "decade's worth of medical advice was misguided", on low fat diets. Interestingly, the researchers find that none of the diets works very well and a year after being on diets on an average people lost only five kilograms. A hardly impressive figure for the effort needed to comply to strict diets. It may sound small but experts say it does medically benefit the patient.

When confronted with a choice on the dining table should one opt for a low fat but high carbohydrate option like having the south Indian delicacy *Idli* or tuck in fried '*puri* and *kachori*'. A new study published in *The Lancet: Diabetes & Endocrinology* suggests that "evidence does not support low-fat diets over other dietary interventions for long-term weight loss". If the latest study is to be believed, the latter would do no more or less harm in the long run.

Experts say Indian obesity is linked to carbohydrate intake as compared to obesity in Western countries that is linked to large consumption of fats.

This huge analysis spearheaded by scientists from the Harvard Medical School in Boston carefully sifted through at data from 53 published weight loss studies that included more than 68,000 people and it has found that despite their popularity low fat diets are no more effective than surprise high fat diets in the long-term for effective weight loss.

"Low fat diets are no better than high fat diets", concurs Dr. Ambrish Mithal, Head of Endocrinology and Diabetes Division of the Vedanta Hospital, Gurgaon who says what really matters is 'what goes in and what gets burnt'.

India stares at huge epidemic of obesity a new study by the Indian Council of Medical Research (ICMR) finds. A landmark study found that nearly 13% of the 1.2 billion population could be suffering from obesity. The India Diabetes Study (INDIAB) was spearheaded by the ICMR finds that a huge number 153 million that is comparable to the half the population of USA could be suffering from abdominal obesity or what is colloquially called having a large paunch or a pear-shaped body.

If one needs to maintain low body mass, then Mithal says what matters most is that one burns more calories than consumes. Towards that, a low fat diet may seem attractive since fats have a lot more stored energy as compared to carbohydrates. However, on the flip side Mithal says people on low fat diets end up eating more carbohydrates to satiate their appetites. Compliance becomes a huge problem. Indian diets are high on calories and low on fibres, V. Mohan a specialist on diabetes from Chennai says rice accounts for almost half of the calorific intake in Indians. Polished rice is mostly carbohydrates.

Concurring with the findings of *The Lancet (D&E)* is Ishi Khosla, one of India's best-known nutrition and dietary habits experts who says "the relevance of low fat diet shifted for over two decades in clinical practice in favour of low carbohydrate diets and good fats. This was prompted by the recognition of the benefits of high fat Mediterranean diets and the French paradox. This in fact was more relevant in the Indian population burdened with the epidemic of diabetes. Low fat diets are high in carbohydrates which is counterproductive."

Incidentally, most diet plans fared poorly especially when long-term weight loss was measured over more than a one-year period. This is probably because people getting into a diet plan follow it rather strictly in the beginning but as time passes they start consuming the same amount of calories and start gaining weight.

Mithal says the large public health message from the huge study is rather simple if you have to lose weight, eat fewer calories and burn them and a balanced diet helps to that faster as compared to trying to stick by the current fad of sticking to 'low fat' diets.

November 15, 2015

□

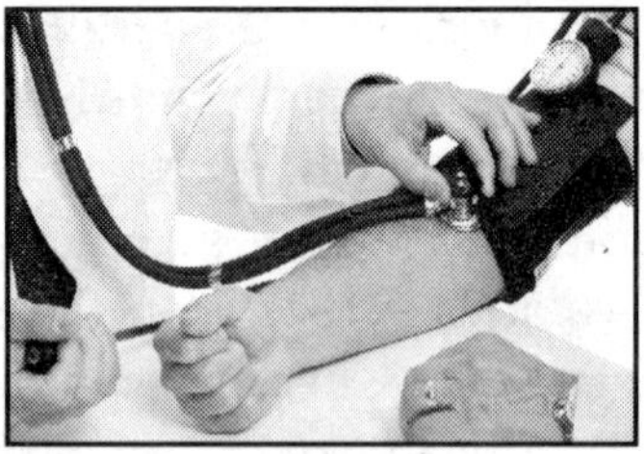

16

WHO Urges India to be Vigilant, as a New Deadly 'Camel Virus' Shakes the Soul of Seoul City

A new virus has shaken Seoul, the capital of South Korea, now it is creeping closer to India. A relatively new lethal 'camel virus' technically called the Middle East Respiratory Syndrome Corona Virus or MERS has taken a huge toll on the confidence of the South Koreans.

The World Health Organisation (WHO) has urged India to be vigilant about a possible attack by the virus that is spreading fast. A top WHO official Dr. Poonam Khetrapal Singh, Regional Director, WHO South-East Asia Region, New Delhi urged India "to enhance surveillance for severe acute respiratory infections, focus on early diagnosis, and step up infection prevention and control procedures in health-care facilities". She triggered an alarm by saying "Strong health systems using strict infection control measures would be the key to prevent the spread of the virus and protect health-care workers and others".

In South Korea, the epidemic continues. The economy of Seoul considered the fourth largest in the world with an annual GDP of $845 billion is taking a hit because of the tinniest creatures of the world. This new pathogen is very similar to the virus that causes the 'common cold' yet so deadly that almost a third of the patients infected with this new virus have died. No specific treatment or a vaccine is available against this new disease.

Many people on the streets of Seoul are wearing surgical masks, such was the demand that chemist shops ran out of supplies. When one lands at the airport, special screening procedures and a health quarantine facility screen all incoming passengers.

A high level panel of the WHO convened to assess this current emergency pointed to several factors that could led to the outbreak, which included a lack of awareness among health-care workers and the general public about MERS; a suboptimal infection prevention and control measures in hospitals; close and prolonged contact of infected MERS patients in crowded emergency rooms and hospital wards with many beds to a room; the custom of many visitors or family members staying with infected patients in the hospital rooms facilitated secondary spread of infections among contacts.

These conditions are all too familiar for us in India so it is a surprise that the virus has still not spread to India so far, since huge numbers of workers travel to the Middle Eastern countries. It is estimated that they send remittances of over $10 billion annually to India but thankfully none have brought home the deadly new virus.

In the midst of the rising epidemic, I was to visit Seoul, for participation in the 9th World Conference of Science Journalists and it was my teenage son who alerted me to the threat of the epidemic and asked me to carry face masks. Not, unduly concerned, I decided to heed the advice of the WHO to proceed without fear since there was no spread of the virus within the wider community but was restricted specifically only to infected hospitals of Seoul.

In the 21st century, new viruses are popping up with impunity, from the SARS virus in 2002; Swine Flu in 2009; Bird Flu in 2013; and Ebola in 2014 and now the latest Asian outbreak of MERS in 2015. Globalization is also helping the spread of viruses to new parts of the world at unforeseen speeds.

Fortunately, for India, the deadly camel virus has not found its way into the country despite the huge population of over six million expatriate workers earning a living in the Gulf countries the epicentre of the MERS virus. There have been fears that the MERS virus could find its way to India through pilgrims returning after the Haj pilgrimage later.

This deadly virus was inadvertently imported into South Korea on May 20, 2015 and since then over 160 cases have been reported with at least 24 people losing their lives. The country's best known hospital the Samsung Medical Centre in Seoul with nearly 2000 beds and treating almost 8000 patients a day has almost been shut down as it became the epicentre of the Korean MERS epidemic. This high tech facility comparable to the All India Institute of Medical Sciences (AIIMS) of New Delhi failed to take suitable and necessary precautions and became the hot bed for new infections in South Korea. A worker returning from Bahrain brought in the virus to South Korea and then through a series of blunders by the hospital staff the virus seems to have taken a hold in this bustling city of 10 million people.

An infected person develops common symptoms like a cough, has fever a shortness of breath with a sensation of vomiting and in severe cases it causes a pneumonia and kidney failure. Recording the medical and travel case history is crucial in trying to diagnose the disease.

Viruses are often described as 'a piece of bad news wrapped up in a protein', and these are so small that world's best microscopes are used to view them. These tiny creatures are so smart that they commandeer the life support systems of human cells to literally make it to dance to their tunes.

The original host of MERS virus is supposed to be

camels and in 2012, it first showed up in Saudi Arabia and since then over 1200 cases have been reported worldwide and about 500 people have died because of this new infection. The virus has a high mortality rate of 36%.

In Seoul, it was the crowded conditions of the emergency rooms and a failure to adhere to standard safety precautions when dealing with a highly infectious disease led to its rapid multiplication. A peculiar habit of Koreans called 'doctor shopping', where patients hop from facility to facility and from doctor to doctor seeking second opinions exacerbated the situation. Most of the infected are people who have come in direct contact of the infected patient at a point when the person is suffering from severe sickness conditions. It has been puzzling doctors as to why new infections were taking place only in hospital settings, said Sung-Han Kim, an Associate Professor, Department of Infectious Diseases, Asan Medical Center, Seoul who added that "patients are non-infective in the two week incubation period but become infective only when the symptoms become so severe that the patients need urgent medical attention". While little is known about the new disease, it is suggested that the viral load in severely infected patients becomes so high that they can easily transmit the disease to care-givers and hence medical workers in South Korea were the new foci of infections.

The WHO in its assessment expressed that this outbreak in South Korea "is a wake-up call and that in a highly mobile world, all countries should always be prepared for the unanticipated possibility of outbreaks of this, and other serious infectious diseases." Is India's health ministry taking suitable precautions? At least at the Indira Gandhi International Airport none were visible, even though the alarm has been sounded.

June 20, 2015

□

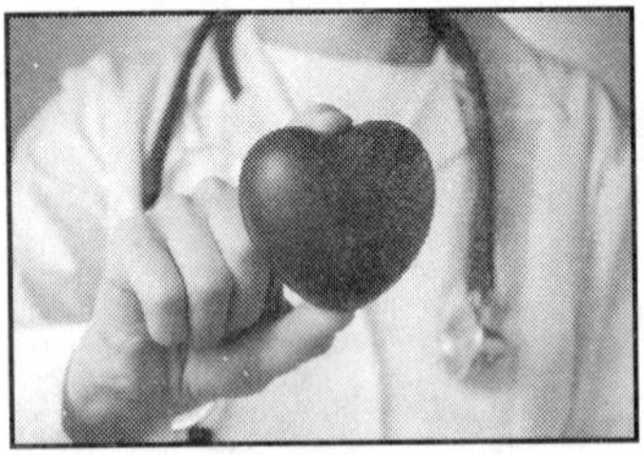

17

Mobile Phones, White Coats and Neckties all Part of a Doctor's Attire Spread Dangerous Infections

The ever-present mobile phones are a source of spreading infections in health-care settings, as they are almost never sterilized. New evidence also suggests that the familiar white coat and neckties that physicians and doctors wear in India should be banned, as they are also potential sources of infection. Diseases spread through such routes are called 'hospital-acquired infections' and such illnesses are really hard to treat as these germs are usually very hardy as they have survived the hostile hospital environments.

Studies indicate that even the ubiquitous mobile phone also tend to harbour infections as they are almost never disinfected by health-care workers, a recent Australian study found that five per cent of the mobile phones they analysed were source of disease causing bacteria. Mobile since they come in close contact with the body become infected with germs.

Most doctors it seems wear white coats and neckties more like ornaments to look 'professional' a study suggests. 'Do doctors need to wear white coats at all?' questions Edmond Fernandes, working at the Department of Community Medicine, Yenepoya Medical College, Mangalore. Writing in the latest issue of the *British Medical Journal* (*BMJ*), he says "today we know white coats harbour potential contaminants and contribute considerably to the burden of disease acquired in hospital by spreading infections". Often potent 'superbugs' pass from patient to patient as the health-care workers go about their daily jobs. Simple hand washing can reduce chances of infections but those bacteria and viruses that are hitched onto the physician's clothes are easy to pass on to other patients as doctors make their rounds in hospitals.

A Turkish study found that almost 95% of the mobile phones of health-care workers were contaminated with different bacteria some of them were antibiotic resistant and highly infectious. Similarly, a 2009 study from the Sri Ramachandra Medical College and Research Institute in Chennai found that about 71% of the mobiles phones of health-care workers were spreading infections. To their horror, they found that only 12% of the doctors ever wiped their mobile phones with disinfectants. Padma Srikanth from the Department of Microbiology who led the study says the 'high level of contamination is disturbing', who dubs them as an 'emerging threat for infection control'.

A 2012 study at the Bangalore Medical College and Research Institute found that none of the medical students they surveyed washed their aprons daily and more than 80% washed their white coats only once a week. This according to the study published in the *Journal of Clinical* and *Diagnostic Research* led to the white coats 'harbouring infections'. They reported that some deadly pathogens like antibiotic resistant strains of the commonly found bacteria *Staphylococcus aureus* and *Pseudomonas aeruginosa* were found on the laboratory white coats worn by the medical students.

Asima Banu, from the Bowring and Lady Curzon Hospital, Bengaluru who did the survey found that medical students who were residing at home tended to have white coats that were more contaminated as compared to students who were residing in hostels. This Banu says "was a worrying prospect, as hospital organisms were likely to spread in the community" so ironically doctors become a threat to health of the public.

On similar lines, a 2010 Irish study found that "it is poor practice to wear neckties (other than bowties) in any care activity that involves contact with patients, as they serve no beneficial function in patient care and are rarely laundered". This study published in the *BMJ* from the Department of Clinical Microbiology, St Vincent's University Hospital, Dublin, Ireland found that "forty per cent of the neckties were contaminated".

Making a plea to shed the white coats Fernandes says since in Indian hospitals changing areas are rare so most doctors tend to wear white coats outside hospitals as well or often leave them on chairs, often students wear them even to the cafeteria and shopping malls. "Given India's tropical climate, common sense indicates that wearing of white coats should be discouraged", especially long-sleeved ones as they are most prone to be infected.

An estimate in the *New England Journal of Medicine* suggests that in USA alone annually some 1.7 million people get affected by hospital-acquired infections and out of these some 99,000 annually succumb to such infections. Comparable Indian estimates are hard to come by but hospital-based infections are frequent in India.

Looking at the scenario, the *BMJ* report seeks that the Indian Ministry of Health should "ban doctors medical students from wearing white coats, to reduce the harm and cost that results from hospital-acquired infections". Protocols need to be put in place that mandates doctors and nurses sterilize their mobile phones.

Howsoever will doctors be willing to disinfect their

mobile phones and would they change their traditional attire and more importantly will the patients ever take their physicians to be serious professionals minus their white coats.

July 26, 2015

□

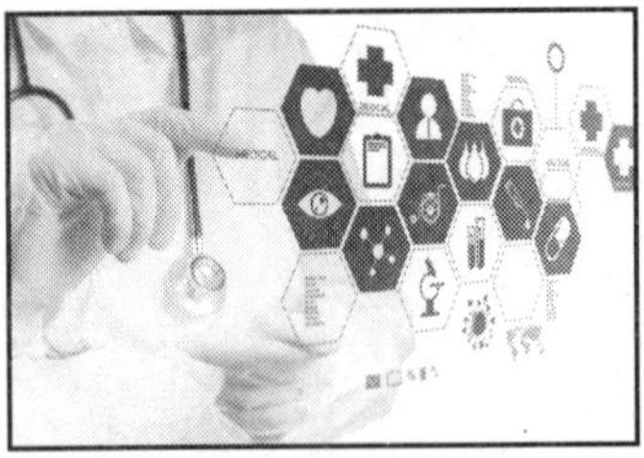

18

India could be Hit by a Tsunami of Obesity!

India stares at huge epidemic of obesity, a new study by the Indian Council of Medical Research (ICMR) finds. A landmark study finds that nearly 13% of the 1.2 billion population could be suffering from obesity. This is ironical since until recently the discourse was mostly about rampant malnourishment in the country. Now it seems India is being hi tat both ends of the spectrum. The multi-hospital 16-person research team says "undernutrition due to poverty which dominated in the past, is being rapidly replaced by obesity associated with affluence."

Obesity or being highly overweight is an avoidable health condition and it can be a precipitating factor for many debilitating lifestyle diseases like diabetes, hypertension, heart disease, and strokes. Dr. Rajendra Pradeepa from the Madras Diabetes Research Foundation, Chennai and the lead author of the study quips "the longer the waist belt the shorter is the lifetime!".

The main causes for rising obesity in India the ICMR-funded study attributes is to increasing urbanisation, use of mechanized transport, consumption of fast foods, long hours of television viewing and the intake of energy dense but nutrient poor diets. High blood pressure, high blood sugar among others are the "leading causes of health loss in

India at present" says Dr. Soumya Swaminathan, Director General of the ICMR.

The India Diabetes Study (INDIAB) was spearheaded by the ICMR finds that a huge number 153 million that is comparable to the half the population of USA could be suffering from abdominal obesity or what is colloquially called having a large paunch or a pear-shaped body. In this study, a man is considered to be obese if the waist circumference is more than 90 centimetres and a woman is obese if the waist is more than 80 centimetres. The startling finding is that as many as 88 million people could be overweight who could sooner than later tip over and become obese with time. Without sounding too alarmist it means that almost a fifth of Indians are carrying more weight than they should.

On the same lines, a new study published the latest issue of *The Lancet* on health risks finds "fewer Indians are having health loss from ailments associated with childhood undernutrition and unsafe water sources, but more Indians are having health loss from diseases attributable to high blood pressure, high blood sugar and high cholesterol".

There could be an overlap in numbers and the ICMR study finds that as many as 107 million Indians, which is equal to the population of Philippines, could suffer from combined obesity. While another 135 million, which is equal to the entire population of Japan could be suffering from generalized obesity. All of these conditions are susceptible to contracting many forms of lifestyle diseases.

It is like 'an impending tsunami', says Dr. Gautam Ahluwalia from the Department of Medicine, Dayanand Medical College, Ludhiana who says the study finds that "less than ten per cent of people in India performed recreational physical activity", this lack of exercise is the root cause for many of the lifestyle-related health problems. Ahluwalia adds that "India is being confronted with the phenomenon of double burden of disease", like infectious illnesses on one hand and non-communicable diseases like lifestyle-related problems on the other hand.

The 16-member team of researchers intensively surveyed some 16,000 individuals in Tamil Nadu, Maharashtra, Jharkhand and Chandigarh and they have published the results of the first phase of their work in the latest issue of the reputed *Indian Journal of Medical Research* (*IJMR*), the big India numbers are an extrapolation. When the entire study is completed in three years, the sample size would jump to 124,000 people making it the largest study of its kind ever to be undertaken. The sample includes residents of both rural and urban areas. On expected lines, the prevalence of obesity was higher in urban populations as compared to rural populations but the worrying fact is that the curve has an upward swing with numbers likely to increase. The study implicates higher levels of obesity with the higher consumption of wheat and rice in daily diets as compared to diets that are rich in millets.

According to the World Health Organisation (WHO), every sixth individual on Earth is obese and some 2.8 million individuals die every year because of obesity and today, "obesity is being recognised as a disease itself".

"Metabolic risk factors that include high blood pressure, blood sugar and cholesterol, along with unhealthy dietary habits and smoking are responsible for about 5.2 million premature deaths in India every year," confirms Dr. K. Srinath Reddy who is President of the Public Health Foundation of India, Gurgaon who adds "This trend will continue to increase unless effective prevention strategies to address these risk factors are implemented in India rapidly."

There is a highly counter-intuitive finding in the study; the more educated suffer from higher levels of obesity. Ahluwalia says "the increasing trend of obesity with increasing education status is paradoxical". Highlighting that "possibly higher education with its increasing economic sovereignty results in higher consumption of obesogenic foods and a sedentary lifestyle".

Leading Indian diabetes specialist Dr. Ambrish Mithal who is Head of Endocrinology and Diabetes Division of Vedanta Hospital Gurgaon says "the big challenge India faces is the burgeoning epidemic of childhood obesity. Linked to greater affluence and urbanisation, obesity fuels an epidemic of non-communicable diseases like diabetes, hypertension and heart disease. The exponential increase in diabetes, especially among the youth, with its attendant complications can be directly attributed to increasing obesity. The challenge is huge we need 'upstream' strategies like greater awareness regarding diet and exercise and, even more importantly, availability of healthy food options for youngsters at schools and their workplace."

"This is really a wake-up call" says Pradeepa who says today the take-off age for obesity has reduced to the 25-34 age group which is 'very worrying' and policy-makers should address this on an urgent basis else obesity could well become the number one killer for the country.

September 13, 2015

□

19

What Ails India? A New Study finds on any Given Day about 35 Million Indians could be Unwell!

What ails India? This is not a rhetorical question seeking a debate on secularism or intolerance but a genuine medical question that has baffled researchers. Interestingly, there are only guestimates and well-researched studies have never been undertaken. Now the first results from a doctor certified database is throwing new light on what really ails India. It seems the toxic air of India is giving breathing difficulties to many Indians.

When results of this landmark study are extrapolated, it means that on any given day about 35 million people visit a doctor and just to give a comparative figure this is equal to the entire population of Canada or the combined population of the big four metros, New Delhi, Mumbai, Bengaluru and Chennai. Sundeep Salvi, a lead researcher from the Chest Research Foundation, Pune says "this is an astounding number of people who are unwell in India".

The researchers report that "of the world's 7.5 billion population in 2015, 1.2 billion people live in India. Around 18% of all global deaths and 20% of loss of global disability-adjusted life years (DALYs) occur in India, making it a country with one of the highest disease burdens in the world. Non-communicable diseases have recently overtaken communicable diseases as the leading causes of mortality and morbidity in India."

The new study finds that more than half of the patients who report to medical facilities do so for ailments related to the respiratory system. Extrapolated it could mean that more than half of India finds itself battling breathing and lung related illnesses. A staggering number indeed! However, looking at the dangerous levels of outdoor and indoor air pollution that prevail over India this may well be correct. Recently, Prakash Javadekar Minister of State (Independent Charge) of Environment, Forest and Climate Change echoed similar sentiments when he said "environmental pollution on account of air pollution causes respiratory diseases in children. Air Pollution in general causes respiratory ailments and also may affect lung function. Asthma, chronic obstructive pulmonary disease, chronic bronchitis etc. are the diseases caused by exposure to increasing air pollution. Air pollution is known to be one of the aggravating factors for many respiratory ailments and cardiovascular diseases." Salvi blames the 'poor quality of air we breathe' as the leading cause of the respiratory diseases.

In this study, a staggering over two lakh urban patients visiting primary health care providers on a single given day, were closely examined by a team of scientists from the Institute of Genomics and Integrated Biology (IGIB), New Delhi and the Chest Research Foundation, Pune. The study found that more than half the patients reported for lung and breathing-related illnesses. According to the study, other common ailments presented were related to digestive system symptoms (25%); circulatory symptoms (12.5%); skin complaints (9%); and endocrine disorders (6.6%); hypertension (14.52%); obstructive airways diseases (14.51%); and upper respiratory tract infections (12.9%). Salvi says "for the first time we now have a snap shot of what people in India suffer from".

The researchers chose a season neutral date of February 1 in 2011 to conduct this massive study over 880 cities of India. More than 12,000 doctors were involved in this study and the results are published in the December issue of *The Lancet*—Global Health journal.

Sandeep Salvi, the lead scientist from the Chest Research Foundation, Pune says one of the most alarming findings is that about 21% of those reporting high blood pressure or hypertension were people below forty years of age. This Salvi feels 'indicates a high burden' and recommends that blood pressure should be regularly monitored even in the age group of less than forty years. Concurring with the findings, Krishna D. Rao and David H. Peters from the Health Systems Program, Department of International Health, Johns Hopkins University, Baltimore, USA writing an editorial on the research paper suggest "that there are such high rates of hypertension in younger people has important implications for premature death and disability in the most productive years of life, with economic effects that would extend to the families supported by these people." On a similar basis, Anurag Agrawal a co-author of the paper and a researcher at IGIB says that metro cities have higher prevalence of hypertension and that too in the younger age group.

"This is the first time such a national level data" has been collected says Agrawal who says now they are finding a clear linkage when the data from their study is overlaid with penetration and use of liquefied petroleum gas (LPG). Agarwal says there is a distinct fall in lung and breathing-related ailments in geographical regions where LPG distribution is widespread. Salvi suggests this truly mirrors major step taken by Prime Minister Narendra Modi through his 'give it up', initiative where the National Democratic Alliance Government has been urging rich

Indians to give up the subsidy they enjoy on LPG cylinders so that poor households who still cook using wood and coal can benefit. Indoor pollution is increasingly recognised as a huge avoidable menace. Salvi feels merely providing the right cooking fuel can help reduce the disease burden.

Even as the big global conference on containing effects of climate change opens in Paris, this small study from India should ideally spur policy-makers in India to clean up the toxic air that is polluting large parts of India.

November 29, 2015

□

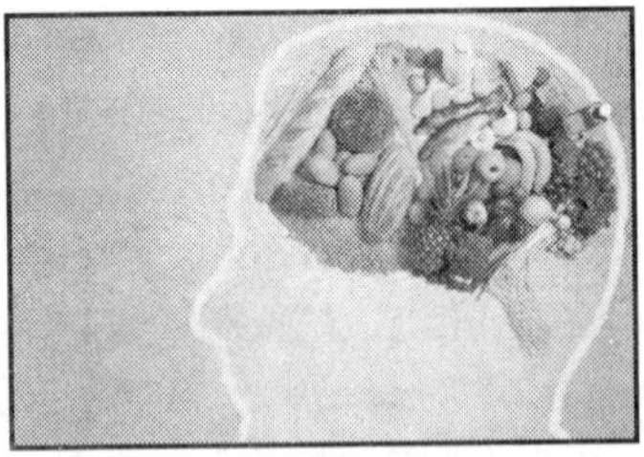

20

ISRO's Rocket Technology to Power Human Hearts

Rocket science may not be able to fix broken hearts, but very soon technology mastered at the Indian Space Research Organisation (ISRO) may be able to help patients who are in need for a heart transplant. Materials and mechanisms used on Indian rockets have been tweaked by ISRO to make a device which some describe as step towards the making of an 'artificial heart'.

ISRO saving the lives of terminally ill patients, the heart assist device has been tested on animals and has been found to be successful. Better known for orbiting satellites and flying giant rockets the multitalented team at ISRO made this heart pump as a spin off technology development in the spare time. Cardiologists are very excited with this development as it offers a lease of life to terminally ill patients since heart transplant still remains out of reach for most and hence a rarity.

Using materials and know how perfected to make lightweight rockets and satellites, scientists at ISRO have perfected a device that assists the human heart to pump blood especially in cases where the left ventricle the most powerful part of a human heart starts to fail. Called the 'left ventricular assist device', this small electrical device can pump 3-5 litres of blood every minute. Kiran Kumar, the

Chairman of ISRO said this rocket technology offered an alternate system to pump blood in very ill patients and it can definitely save human lives.

The special pump made by the Indian space agency can also be powered using an indigenously made highly energy dense battery the Lithium Ion Cell that has also for the first time been made in India again by another team of rocket scientists.

The pump, which weighs about 100 grams can be fitted inside the body or can be placed externally and needs a hook up to a battery to power it.

Made from a special alloy of titanium the device is 'bio-compatible' says K. Sivan, Director of the Vikram Sarabhai Space Center (VSSC), in Thiruvananthapuram it is here that the special heart pump has been mastered. Rocket scientists at VSSC use titanium alloys for making rocket engines and satellite components as consequence they have total mastery on the metallurgy and manufacturing of the material. The same material that is flown on rocket engines has been remodelled to make the compact but high tech pump.

Sivan says "we have seen that the device is meeting all the biomechanical requirements, and the pumping requirement. This particular device was tested on six animals. It was tested for six hours, and after that, the other organs of the animal were checked. They were intact. This is a very great achievement. It's a successful device. Definitely it is a major step towards the ultimate development of an artificial heart by ISRO."

The device pumps blood using a common technology called a centrifugal pump. The electronics and the magnets used in the tiny pump have been fabricated by the same engineers who make lightweight systems used on Indian satellites. The pump had to designed in such a fashion that even with continuous operation it should not heat up and should obviously be fail-proof.

The device which is akin to an artificial heart has been tested on half a dozen pigs. Cardiologists at the Sree Chitra Tirunal Institute for Medical Sciences and Technology (SCTMST) in Thiruvananthapuram surgically operated healthy pigs and replaced the functioning of the left ventricle of the pig with this special pump developed by ISRO. The pig survived a full six hours, which was the full design of the experiment. No damage was reported to the blood as it was pumped by the device after it had bypassed the biological heart, even the other organs of the pig suffered no damage for the full duration of the experiment.

Scientists at (SCTMST) say 'this remains a work in progress' and further experimentation will done on animals before the device can be tried on humans. Wealthy Indian patients needing a heart transplant but unable to get the matching donors already import these devices and some of these left ventricular assist devices have already been installed on patients at some private hospitals and even at the All India Institute of Medical Sciences, New Delhi.

Importing a heart pump device and then implanting it costs over a crore of rupees says cardiologists familiar with the technology, in contrast, scientists at VSSC say the device developed by them cost just ₹ 1.25 lakhs. The rocket scientists say the cost differential is so large simply because the expertise and the materials already existed at VSSC and all they had to do was to assemble the right team of specialists that included metallurgists, electronics engineers, specialists on flow mechanics and designers who worked alongside cardiologists to come up with a suitable design. It took a team of about two dozen specialists about six years and after many permutation and combination, they came up with the right design.

"It is a complicated device to make and this is an exciting development" says Dr. Balram Bhargava, Professor of Cardiology, and Executive Director, Stanford India

Biodesign Centre, School of International Biodesign, All India Institute of Medical Sciences, New Delhi who confirms that no one in India has till date to the best of his knowledge designed indigenously a left ventricular assist device, he adds that it is an important bridge for patients awaiting a heart transplant. Bhargava cautions that the device is to be used only in very specific medical circumstances.

Interestingly, VSSC has also very recently developed high value Lithium Ion Battery which could now be used to power the heart pump. India has all along been importing these Lithium Ion Cells but recently the Transport Minister Nitin Gadkari mandated ISRO to master this technology so that it can be used to power zero pollution electric vehicles. Sivan says VSSC will try to miniaturise these Lithium Ion Cells which can hopefully power the left ventricular assist device.

April 20, 2016

□

21

Health Ministry's Own Survey Projects a Bleak Picture

A far from healthy picture emerges of India when one carefully analyses data on country's health that was released by the government. While there have been gains in the last ten years, large gaps remain that need to be plugged if the dream of having a *'Swachh, Swasthya Bharat'*, has to become a reality soon.

A landmark survey released by the Ministry of Health and Family Welfare presents a somewhat bleak picture of India's health.

The survey a quick but robust snap shot of India's health was revealed as part of the National Family Health Survey-4 (NFHS-4), presents data for 13 states and two union territories. Data for rest of the country is expected to be released later in the year.

In its report', the Health Ministry asserts that "fewer children are dying in infancy and early childhood", yet some startling results emerge when the data is carefully teased out.

The latest survey suggests that "wasting or severe malnutrition in children is still very high by international standards" in all of the 13 states and two union territories that were surveyed and to put it in perspective according to UNICEF the prevalence of underweight children in India remains double that of Sub-Saharan Africa with 62 million children under the age of five being stunted.

According to UNICEF, "in India, almost half of children younger than five years of age are stunted, a manifestation of chronic undernutrition. Stunting and other forms of under-nutrition are thought to be responsible for nearly half of all child deaths globally. Stunting is associated with an under developed brain, with long-lasting harmful consequences, including diminished mental ability and learning capacity, poor school performance in childhood, reduced earnings and increased risks of nutrition-related chronic diseases, such as diabetes, hypertension, and obesity in future." While India's economy has been growing at impressive rate, the country still has the highest number of stunted children in the world. Stunting starts from pre-conception when an adolescent girl and who later becomes mother is undernourished and anaemic; it worsens when infants diets are poor, and when sanitation and hygiene is inadequate. It is irreversible by the age of two. Child survival and health is inseparably connected to reproductive and, maternal health. As high as 70% of adolescent girls in India are anaemic.

Shri J.P. Nadda, Union Minister for Health and Family Welfare speaking at the release of the 'India Health Report: Nutrition 2015', admitted that "despite positive changes we have a continuing problem of undernutrition, which means that our children may survive due to better health and vaccines but may not reach their full potential as productive citizens."

The NFHS-4 survey says "in Bihar, Madhya Pradesh and Meghalaya more than 40% of children are stunted." Today, India accounts for 33% of stunted children in the world. According to UNICEF, 48% of children under-five years in India are stunted. Which means every second child has not grown to the best of his/her capabilities. 'Hidden hunger' is taking a big toll on the health of Indian's emphasizes Dr.

M.S. Swaminathan, well-known agriculturist also dubbed the 'Father of the Green Revolution', who says 'micro-nutrient deficiency' is plaguing the country.

"Since the last report in 2005-06 the survey indicates 'anaemia has declined but still remains widespread. More than half of children are anaemic in ten of the 15 states and union territories. More than half of women are anaemic in eleven states and union territories."

The Health Ministry says the situation of immunisation has 'substantially improved' since a decade ago. Yet the latest survey indicates that about 40% of the children do not get a full immunization cover. To bridge the gap, the Prime Minister Narendra Modi-led National Democratic Alliance Government in 2015 launched *'Mission Indhradhanush'* to achieve better coverage of immunisation. According to Nadda, this initiative "aims to cover all those children by 2020 who are either unvaccinated, or are partially vaccinated against seven vaccine preventable diseases which include diphtheria, whooping cough, tetanus, polio, tuberculosis, measles and hepatitis B."

Taking a swipe at the performance of the last government led by Prime Minister Manmohan Singh, Nadda recently said "between 2009-13 immunization coverage has increased from 61% to 65%, indicating only 1% increase in coverage every year. To accelerate the process of immunization by covering 5% and more children every year, the mission mode has been adopted to achieve target of full coverage by 2020."

On vaccination, a great positive is that India has continued to be free of the wild polio virus for the fifth year in the running. However, complacency can easily erode those gains. Dr. Poonam Khetrapal Singh, Regional Director for World Health Organisation's South-East Asia Regional Office in New Delhi asserts "we need to ensure that our efforts and investment over the years to eradicate polio do not go waste. Globally, polio transmission is at its lowest ever levels. However, the risk of importation of the polio virus into all polio-free areas persists."

Interestingly, the survey also reflects the dichotomy of the country. "Over nutrition continues to be a health issue for adults. At least three in ten women are overweight or obese in Andaman and Nicobar Islands, Andhra Pradesh, Goa, Puducherry, and Tamil Nadu" the survey reports.

When air pollution both indoor and outdoor has been dominating the headlines, the survey finds that "only 18% of households in Bihar use of clean cooking fuel, which reduces the risk of respiratory illness and pollution'."

The 13 states covered in the NFHS-4 survey include Andhra Pradesh, Bihar, Goa, Haryana, Karnataka, Madhya Pradesh, Meghalaya, Sikkim, Tamil Nadu, Telangana, Tripura, Uttarakhand, West Bengal, and the two Union Territories of Andaman and Nicobar Islands and Puducherry. Rest of states will be covered in phases and finally about 570,000 households will be surveyed.

Among the other gains, the health ministry reports that after the last round of National Family Health Survey in 2005-06, infant mortality has declined in all first phase States/Union Territories for which trend data are available. All 15 States/Union Territories have rates below 51 deaths per 1,000 live births, although there is considerable variation among the States/Union Territories. Infant mortality rates range from a low of 10 in Andaman and Nicobar Islands to a high of 51 deaths per 1000 live births in Madhya Pradesh. Better care for women during pregnancy and childbirth contributes to reduction of maternal deaths and improved child survival.

There is huge unmet challenge in health stares India as the country aspires to become a developed country at the earliest.

June 19, 2016

□

22

Taming a Tiny Terrorist called TB, Indian Scientists Provide New Insights for Drug Discovery

There is deadly terrorist out there and it kills about 1000 people every day in India which is almost one person every minute. No jail is strong enough to contain this tiny beast and it has found its way in half of India's population and is ready to strike as and when the guard of the body is lowered. This fierce killer called the tuberculosis bacterium does not wield a Kalashnikov rifle but its slow poison infects about five lakh Indians every year making them fall prey to TB.

To take care of more than half a billion people who could fall prey to TB, the government has allocated a mere ₹ 1640 crores. A mere drop in the ocean to contain this deadly terrorist. In contrast the Indian Government hopes to spend over ₹ 58,000 crores to buy 36 Rafale Fighter Jets. Each fighter jets costs almost the same amount India spends annually to treat five lakh TB patients.

In this war on TB, all hope is not lost now researchers from the Indian Institute of Science, Bengaluru have managed to break into TB bacterium's highly secure intelligence gathering mechanism which senses the drugs being used to attack this slow growing organism. The hope being if one understands how the TB bacterium becomes drug resistant discovering drugs that can kill it may be that much easier.

To strike at the root of any terrorist organisation getting reliable insider information is key to busting it and then eliminating it. Similar is the case with the dodgy TB bacteria that just stealthily hides away in our bodies and strikes when it sees an opportunity.

Now, Deepak Kumar Saini an Assistant Professor at the Department of Molecular Reproduction, Development and Genetics, Indian Institute of Science, Bengaluru is deciphering the signalling mechanism within the TB bacterium which gives it this invincibility. How does the TB bacterium figure out that a new drug is being used to kill it and how this organism that has existed at least since Biblical times manages to become drug resistant.

To use an analogy from Indian mythology, in the sacred text of *Ramayana* it is stated that the Lankan Lord Ravana the demon king was almost invincible and only an insider knew his weakness on what strategy to adopt to kill him. Ravana's impregnable defence and its weakness were known only to his immediate family. Insider information being leaked to Lord Rama led to the killing of Ravana. In the same fashion, it is insider information on the biochemical pathways as to what is happening within the TB bacterium can help unravel the chinks in its armoury to fell this tiny terrorist.

The TB bacterium is cunning and is able to survive according to the researchers due to its ability to sense and adapt to its host's environment. Saini's laboratory is working at unravelling the molecular mechanism that helps the tuberculosis bacterium sense, respond and adapt to its host environment.

In a recent research paper, Saini says starting with the basics, for any sensory system to function, there has to be a minimum of two components with one receiving the signals and then subsequently transferring the signal to another component. Two-component signalling, as the name suggests has two protein components involved in the signalling. The first is a 'receptor' molecule called the Sensor Kinase (SK), which is present on the outer membrane surrounding cells and is responsible for 'receiving' diverse environmental stimuli. The second component is the 'effector' molecule called the Response Regulator (RR), which when activated by the Sensor Kinase (SK) produces an 'effect', by binding to specific regions of the bacterial DNA and activating the decoding of genes involved, in the response to that stimulus. "One can, therefore, appreciate the extreme importance of these systems for the pathogen", explains Saini. "Without these systems, the pathogen will not be able to adapt and survive inside the hostile and constantly changing host environment. Understanding signalling systems like the two component system may be the key to combating this pathogen more effectively", he adds.

The TB bacterium has also been evolving as humans fight it, in the first instance four front line drugs are deployed to treat TB, occasionally since the treatment of TB is a prolonged one lasting several months, patients often abandon the intake of antibiotics halfway. This gives the organism an opportunity to develop resistance and becomes multi-drug resistant, some 79,000 people have been detected with MDR-TB reports the health ministry. In rare cases, it becomes even more virulent and is classed as extremely drug-resistant TB and about 2700 such cases have been reported. Further of late some totally drug-resistant strains of the TB bacterium have also been detected.

Reacting to this alarming situation, Shri J.P. Nadda, Union Minister of Health and Family Welfare said "The Government of India stands committed to accelerating its efforts to combat tuberculosis in the country".

Recently, the Health Ministry launched Bedaquiline—new anti-TB drug for treating-drug resistant TB. The drug is a new anti-TB drug for treatment of MDR-TB. This new class of drug specifically targets Mycobacterial ATP synthase, an enzyme essential for supply of energy to Mycobacterium tuberculosis and most other mycobacteria. This drug is indicated for use in the treatment of drug-resistant TB. Incidentally, one of the co-discoverers of the drug is Dr. Anil Koul, a Kashmiri Pandit who fled the valley at the height of the insurgency and now works in Belgium. Terrorists made Koul migrate out of J&K but then he chased his dream of trying to find a cure for this tiny bacterial terrorist.

All efforts are needed to thwart this microscopic terrorist that threatens India, this novel approach at understanding the signalling pathways of the TB bacterium offers an "exciting new way to try and contain the TB epidemic", says Saini.

July 10, 2016

□

23

Failing Antibiotics: The World Wakes Up to the Worst Horror!

At UN, global leaders commit to act on antimicrobial resistance collective effort to address a challenge to health, food security, and development 21 September 2016, New York—World leaders today signalled an unprecedented level of attention to curb the spread of infections that are resistant to antimicrobial medicines.

Antimicrobial resistance (AMR) happens when bacteria, viruses, parasites and fungi develop resistance against medicines that were previously able to cure them.

For the first time, Heads of State committed to taking a broad, coordinated approach to address the root causes of AMR across multiple sectors, especially human health, animal health and agriculture. This is only the fourth time a health issue has been taken up by the UN General Assembly (the others were HIV, non-communicable diseases and Ebola). The high-level meeting was convened by the President of the 71st Session of the UN General Assembly, H.E. Peter Thomson.

"Antimicrobial resistance threatens the achievement of the Sustainable Development Goals and requires a global response," Mr. Thomson said. "Member States have today agreed upon a strong political declaration that provides a good basis for the international community to move forward. No one country, sector or organization can address this issue alone."

Countries reaffirmed their commitment to develop national action plans on AMR, based on the Global Action Plan on Antimicrobial Resistance—the blueprint for tackling AMR developed in 2015 by the World Health Organization (WHO) in coordination with the Food and Agriculture Organization of the United Nations (FAO) and the World Organization for Animal Health (OIE). Such plans are needed to understand the full scale of the problem and stop the misuse of antimicrobial medicines in human health, animal health and agriculture. Leaders recognized the need for stronger systems to monitor drug-resistant infections and the volume of antimicrobials used in humans, animals and crops, as well as increased international cooperation and funding.

They pledged to strengthen regulation of antimicrobials, improve knowledge and awareness, and promote best practices—as well as to foster innovative approaches using alternatives to antimicrobials and new technologies for diagnosis and vaccines.

"Antimicrobial resistance poses a fundamental threat to human health, development and security. The commitments made today must now be translated into swift, effective, life saving actions across the human, animal and environmental health sectors. We are running out of time," said Dr. Margaret Chan, Director-General of WHO.

Common and life-threatening infections like pneumonia, gonorrhoea and post-operative infections, as well as HIV, tuberculosis and malaria are increasingly becoming untreatable because of AMR. Left unchecked, AMR is predicted to have significant social, health security and economic repercussions that will seriously undermine the development of countries.

The high levels of AMR already seen in the world today are the result of overuse and misuse of antibiotics and other antimicrobials in humans, animals (including farmed fish) and crops, as well as the spread of residues of these medicines in soil, crops and water. Within the broader context of AMR, resistance to antibiotics is considered the greatest and most urgent global risk requiring international and national attention.

"AMR is a problem not just in our hospitals, but on our farms and in our food, too. Agriculture must shoulder its share of responsibility, both by using antimicrobials more responsibly and by cutting down on the need to use them, through good farm hygiene," said Dr. José Graziano da Silva, Director-General of FAO.

"Effective and accessible antibiotics are as vital for protecting animal health and welfare and good veterinary medicine as they are for human health. We urge national authorities to strongly support all sectors involved, through promotion of responsible and prudent use, good practices and implementation of established standards and guidelines," said Dr. Monique Eloit, Director General of OIE.

Leaders at the UN meeting called on WHO, FAO and OIE, in collaboration with development banks such the World Bank other relevant stakeholders, to coordinate their planning and actions and to report back to the UN General Assembly in September 2018.

Countries called for better use of existing, cost-effective tools for preventing infections in humans and animals. These include immunization, safe water and sanitation, and good hygiene in hospitals and animal husbandry. Putting in place systems to ensure more appropriate use of existing and new antibiotics is also essential.

In addition, they highlighted market failures, and called for new incentives for investment in research and development of new, effective and affordable medicines, rapid diagnostic tests and other important therapies to replace those that are losing their power.

They stressed that affordability and access to existing and new antibiotics, vaccines and other medical tools should be a global priority and should take into account the needs of all countries.

September 25, 2016

□

INTERNATIONAL

24

Burgeoning Indo-US Relations: Denial of Visas to Scientists Remains A Big Thorn in the Flesh

Indian and American scientists suggest first name friends 'Barrack and Narendra', should at their summit level iron out the wrinkles that leads to denial and delays for the granting of visas to researchers for travel to both countries.

Despite bonhomie and garden side *'chai-pe-charcha'* between President Barrack Obama and Prime Minister Narendra Modi that formed part of the 'new journey' the two countries embarked upon earlier this year, instances of visa snafus remain a stumbling block. Visa rules remain a bottleneck that impedes free scientific exchange between the world's largest and world's oldest democracies.

Earlier Bharat Ratna Prof. C.N.R. Rao, as science advisor to the Prime Minister had called the American visa regime regressive and demeaning. The jostling is not one-sided, three years back India actually deported a respected earthquake researcher Dr. Roger Bilham after he had landed at New Delhi. The angst is on both sides and it seems boffins are on the receiving end of the entrenched bureaucracies.

Scientists by nature are impatient and would rather spend time in their laboratories understanding the universe than filling up loads of forms and stand in front of 'jail-like' windows giving interviews to more often than not consular individuals who have no clue about science but are slaves of the complex diplomatic legalese. This leads to frustration on all sides and occasionally the scientific pressure cooker tips over.

This week, India's leading petroleum researcher Dr. M.O. Garg, Director General of the Council of Scientific and Industrial Research (CSIR), New Delhi went livid on what he called was a 'denial of granting a US visa', for him to attend a scientific meeting in Columbus, Ohio. Garg heads India's largest network of 38 civilian labs employing over 4000 scientists with an annually budget of about ₹ 3800 crores.

America is not a new country for him, he has travelled more than a dozen times since 1983 and in 1988 he spent more than seven months at a stretch in USA, his last visit was in 2009 so he has traversed the many biometric hoops put in place by the US State Department after 9/11 attacks.

Garg is a genial and jolly scientist not known for angry outbursts, having published more than 250 research papers, holds over 30 patents of which half a dozen are US Patents, all-in-all he is a highly regarded chemist who won't tolerate fools or get pushed around. Well-travelled in the last decade he has had 32 overseas visits from Brazil to Australia. Now this week he had enough from the American bureaucracy.

On June 1, Dr. Garg recounts that he spent almost half a day filling out screen after screen of questions to apply for his US Visa which he calls was like writing down 'my *janam patri* or life history', a day later in usual fashion he was fingerprinted and photographed. On June 3, he was asked to appear for the 'visa interview' which he did at 8.30 am and he recalls that 'questions for which the consular official already had answers', were popped to him which he says he patiently answered. Then it seems his troubles began when he was asked to appear for another face-to-face interview at new window where he was now given a piece of paper with several questions and a 'tracking number'. Dr. Garg says having procured several US visas in the past this now meant to him that he was being 'singled out'. He says even after more than three weeks of waiting the visa was not granted to him. He was to travel to the US on June 15 for which he had already purchased an air ticket and the meeting itself was scheduled for June 17. Till June 24, well after the meeting was over Garg says the visa never came through and he finally had to cancel his trip. Garg says both countries lost an important opportunity to forge stronger scientific ties.

On their part, the US Embassy in New Delhi which seldom responds to individual visa concerns quickly issued a formal statement: "the visa has not been refused, it is in process. We hope he will be able to travel next week. We regret any delay due to the system outage. We hope he will have many more opportunities in the future to further enhance scientific cooperation between India and the U.S." This is hilarious says Dr. Garg "what use is a US visa after the meeting is long over". He does not buy the argument that the 'system outage' on June 9—where by the entire US visa machinery globally went down after a hardware glitch-affected his particular case.

Garg says if US has to become a 'preferred partner', for India then at the highest levels such hurdles should be removed. In fact, he goes on to suggest that possibly in tit for tat manner India should also retaliate by saying "if, suppose, we do the same thing to US scientists, for example if their Secretary of Energy were refused a visa, don't you think the US would have taken revenge on India as well?"

If you think there is pain only for Indians there are many examples of Americans recounting their horror stories like Dr. Jeffrey S. Kargel of the Department of Hydrology & Water Resources, University of Arizona, USA who says "two years ago I applied for a visa to India for highlevel scientific contacts that were invited by the Indian Space Research Organization and encouraged by NASA. After six weeks of trying, we had to go to high levels in the Embassy, and finally I received my visa 48 hours before my departure. It seems that there are two-way bureaucratic problems." He did attend the meeting at an ISRO facility in Ahmedabad.

In 2006, another respected chemist Prof. Goverdhan Mehta then Director of the Indian Institute of Science, Bengaluru was denied a US visa he said he felt "humiliated after the interview where his research credentials were questioned", the then American Ambassador David Mulford tendered an apology and Dr. Mehta's visa was subsequently hand delivered to his home but he vowed never to go to America again. In this diplomatic shadow boxing the real loss was for the world of science.

According to NDTV in 2013, "annoyed with the US visa rules, C.N.R. Rao, the then Science Advisor to Prime Minister, Manmohan Singh threatened to boycott visiting the US. Mr. Rao had been affected by the US visa norms that allow a one-year visa to some Indian scientists, as opposed to the earlier five to ten year multiple entry visa." Clearly unhappy with the annual pilgrimage scientists were forced to make to the American Embassy, Mr. Rao said, "India is getting roughed up by the Americans." Mr. Rao, a frequent visitor to the US for the past 50 years had been hit by the visa norms for three years now. He said, "I find it very insulting to go through this each year. I am sick and tired...may never go to America again after my current visa expires."

Kargel says "the two countries need to fix the visa problems. I hope both India and the U.S. can make visas easier to obtain. Doing so would improve scientific cooperation." Garg who is still smarting from his wounds says "this visa issue is definitely a thorn in the whole process".

As far back as 2013 US President Barack Obama's current Science Advisor John P. Holdren admitted "I understand visas are a problem...we hope to improve." But it seems little has changed for the scientific community that would reduce their travel woes despite the closeness of '*jadoo-ki-jhappies*' or 'warm hugs' between Modi and Obama.

June 27, 2015

□

25

Amazing Molecules with Life-Saving Properties Discovered Literally from the Cold by Indian Biologists

Indian scientists have discovered extraordinary molecules literally from the cold. Recent findings include anti-cancer molecules from organisms in the Antarctica and life-saving anti-freeze molecules from the Arctic environments. All frigid environments where life's boundaries are pushed to the fullest just to survive. A new effort has also been launched by the Ministry of Earth Sciences to look for similar new molecules but from the high altitude Himalayan region.

Life needs special adaptation mechanisms to survive the extreme cold polar environments where the temperatures for most parts of the year can remain well below 0°C and ice and snow remain a reality all the time. Yet even in these hostile environments microorganisms thrive and survive but evolution has provided them with special protective covers that help them tide over the freezing cold and frigid conditions.

Indian expeditions to the Antarctica and the setting up of a specialized institution the National Centre for Antarctica and Ocean Research (NCAOR) in Goa has started yielding some results. Shiv Mohan Singh a scientist at the NCAOR has reported the finding a new molecule called 'thelebolan' that has anti-cancer properties. The molecule was extracted from a fungus 'Thelebolus microsporus', which was collected from the Larseman Hills not far from the Indian permanent station in the Antarctica. The 'thelebolan' molecule has been characterized and it helps stop the multiplication of cancer cells. Along with scientists from the Indian Institute of Technology, Kharagpur, the team is working to understand the full spectrum of the benefits that 'thelebolan' could offer.

Finding novel drugs from plants is not new, this year's Nobel Prize in Physiology and Medicine was awarded to a Chinese researcher Tu You you who discovered a new anti-malaria compound 'artemisinin' from a plant used in traditional Chinese medicine. The Chinese researcher investigated more than 2000 plants before hitting on a blockbuster anti-malarial drug, which has helped save millions of lives. This Nobel Prize has boosted the morale of boffins like Singh.

According to Singh, 'thelobolan' also helps boost immunity and could help people suffering from HIV/AIDS. The fungus when grown can be used as a 'nutraceutical' to boost wellness says Singh who adds that IIT-Kharagpur has made biscuits where the extracts are used and they are being tested in the laboratory. Full-scale exploitation is still far away as clinical trials still need to be undertaken.

Another important discovery from the NCAOR includes the identification of eight new bacterial strains that have anti-freeze properties. This discovery was made from the glaciers in the Arctic region where India has recently set up a field station. The anti-freeze molecules provide the ability to the organisms to survive the extreme cold temperatures where water would freeze killing the bacteria.

The special protective proteins work by either helping to lower the freezing point of water or sometimes help in avoiding the formation of ice crystals. Once ice crystals are formed, it usually leads to death. The anti-freeze compounds have potentially important applications, like in increasing the shelf life of human organs or helping to store blood for longer durations.

Once an organ is harvested from a brain dead person, there is always a scramble to try to get it across soonest from the donor to the recipient. One often hears of green signal free corridors being designated in cities for the transport of a harvested heart to clear way for an ambulance speeding across town from one hospital to another. As it is, in India organ donors are few and far between, so if the shelf life of the donated organs can be increased it could prove to be a boon for many who wait on long waiting lists like for finding suitable matching kidneys.

Singh says the anti-freeze compounds identified by his team in collaboration with the Japanese could prove to be a big boon. Singh collected a broth of bacteria that were growing in very tiny pools of water found on the tops of glaciers in the Arctic region. Harvested from there these bacteria were then grown in the laboratory on a special medium and the anti-freeze proteins were then isolated from these cell cultures.

The small protein has now been sequenced and Singh and his team hopes to clone it into a fast growing yeast so that in the laboratory pilot scale quantities of the special protein can be extracted. Singh finds that this protein provides that special protective cover that are needed to make the bacteria survive the extreme cold environment.

Singh says commercial exploitation of discoveries from the bioresources of the Arctic region has its own challenges as special laws governing the exploitation of global commons are stringent and could hinder in easy commercialisation.

To avoid some of those complications mostly related to biopiracy, Singh and his team has now launched a new effort to look for similar organisms from the high Himalayan glaciers in the Indian region. In the last two years, his team has made four expeditions to high altitude glaciers like Humta and Chota Shingri, samples have already been collected and his team which has according to him works on a small budget of few lakhs of rupees is trying to identify and extract the cryoprotective proteins from the Himalayan microflora.

Singh says if one surveys the ancient Indian texts one finds several mentions of life-saving herbal mixtures. Singh cites one well-known example where in the epic *Ramayan* there is the mention of the use of a *'Sanjeevani buti'* on Lord Ram's brother Laxman after he had fallen unconscious in the long battle with Ravana in Lanka. To resuscitate Laxman, the *Ramayana* cites that Hanuman the trusted aide of Lord Ram had specially flown to the Himalayas to bring back the *'Sanjeevani buti'* when he could not identify the magical plant, the monkey God Hanuman had lifted up the entire mountain so that the ancient physicians or Vaidyas could pluck the special plant. This extract was then given to Laxman who regained consciousness. Singh feels if he is able to discover the anti-freeze compounds from the Himalayan region he could help re-discover what is possibly the lost art of using something akin to the *'Sanjeevani buti'*. A long shot but he says he will devote the rest of his life looking for these magical cures and then validating it through modern science.

On a recent visit to the NCAOR, India's Science Minister Dr. Harsh Vardhan was shown some of these unique findings and he urged the scientists to bring such findings to early commercialisation.

India has been undertaking annual expeditions at a huge cost to the icy cold Antarctica ever since the first expedition was undertaken in 1981. The leader of the first expedition Dr. S.Z. Qasim recently passed away, microbiologists say it would be great tribute to him if and when the first anti-freeze compound is commercialised it should ideally be named after him.

Singh says using these life-saving anti-freeze proteins on humans still remains a distant dream since first trials on animals have to prove that it actually work on higher forms of life, human use could still be a more than a decade away. Singh asserts his small lab of five researchers has made a humble beginning and he hopes bring it to fruition.

November 1, 2015

□

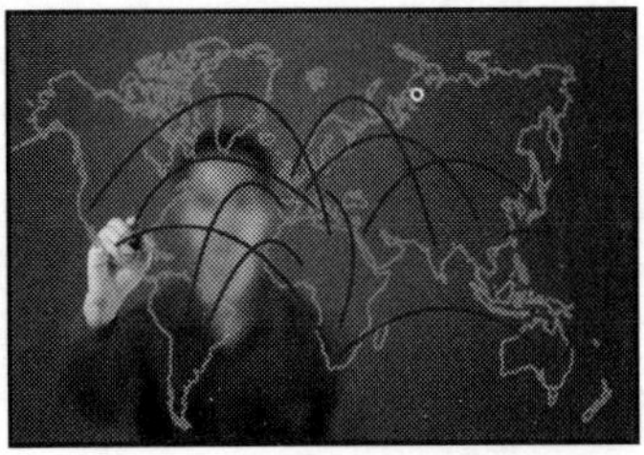

26

'Human Sacrifice' in Shiva's abode Inside the Kingdom of God Particles. Irrational Behaviour by European Scientists Riles India!

Human sacrifice, Lord Shiva's statue, nuclear institute, God Particle, European laboratory in a cavern, mini black holes all makes for a heady mysterious mix. When a creepy grainy video emerges from inside a haloed scientific institution showing a so-called 'human sacrifice' being committed at that global temple of learning where more than 100 nations are cooperating in Geneva called the European Organization for Nuclear Research or CERN, it spooked many. CERN has launched an internal investigation to get to the truth of the matter while confirming the veracity of the video as having been shot within its highly secure premises, but called it a 'fictional' depiction.

This act has riled many scientists especially in India since the 'human sacrifice' is shown being conducted with the backdrop of giant statue of Lord Shiva in his Nataraja pose performing the '*tandava*' or the cosmic dance. The over five meter tall statue was gifted by the Indian Government to the Geneva-based atomic research centre about a decade ago.

CERN is not alone to these acts of irrational behaviour by scientists, it is quite common place in many countries. In USA, engineers at NASA's planetary missions control room invariably eat peanuts when a satellite is being manoeuvred into the Martian orbit, since they believe it brings a good omen. Coconuts are broken by none other than the Prime Minister and his wife to inaugurate a stealth nuclear powered submarine in Vishakhapatnam. The top brass of the Indian Space Research Organisation (ISRO) visit in their 'private time' the temple of Lord Balaji in Tirupati to seek his blessings before a rocket launch and made a habit of placing mini models of the rocket and satellite to the Gods. The fear of the unknown drives many of these irrational behaviours by otherwise highly scientifically-oriented people.

But, what happened at CERN is most bizarre. Against the backdrop of a statue showing the cosmic dance of Lord Shiva a video possibly shot on a mobile phone shows about 6-7 people wearing black satanic cloaks gather in the dead of the night, then another person possibly a lady is seen lying down on a sacrificial bench in front of the Shiva statue, one of the cloaked figures draws a glistening dagger and is shown stabbing the woman. The video is shot as if the eavesdropper was taken by surprise by the happenings they chanced upon and the clip ends with expletives. Whether the video is fictional or real is still a matter of investigation but undoubtedly it was meticulously planned and possibly rehearsed.

Clarifying the position, the spokesperson for CERN said "this video is a work of fiction showing a contrived scene. CERN and its on-site accommodation fills up with scientists from across the world coming to CERN as part of their work. Work at CERN can take place 24 hours a day, 365 days a year with shift work and data analysis. Persons that are authorised to access the CERN site sometimes let their sense of humour go too far, and that is what has happened on this occasion. The video was filmed from an office building; strict safety systems are in place to prevent any unauthorised access to technical and experimental facilities. CERN does not condone this kind of spoof, which breaches CERN's professional guidelines, and is currently carrying out an internal investigation."

Jokes apart, work at CERN conjures up many horrifying images, in 2008 when the world's largest atom smasher was being started up there was an uncalled for global scare that the Large Hadron Collider would generate black holes that could gobble up the earth. It was a global scare but in India it peaked when a 16 year old girl from Madhya Pradesh got so scared that she allegedly committed seeing the news reports. Obviously, the world did not die but reason did, since CERN at that time failed to communicate effectively that its experimentation would not end in a doomsday scenario. Later CERN did make an attempt to bust such myths, but today social media is ablaze with hyped accounts of non-scientific happenings inside the 27 kilometre circular tunnel embedded deep inside the earth and straddling both Switzerland and France which houses the world's human largest experiment.

It was here that the so-called 'God Particle' or the Higgs Boson was discovered in 2013. The mere nick naming of the particle as 'God Particle' makes people believe CERN is trying to prove that God exists. Even though CERN assets "that it exists to understand the mystery of nature for the benefit of humankind."

That India did not erupt on what could be termed as a 'desecration' of venerated iconic Indian God gifted with love by Indian people and placed on an alien soil, only showed that rationality prevailed among the vast Indian masses so prone to being swayed by emotions of religion.

Indian atomic scientists involved with the gifting of the giant Chola Bronze statue were flabbergasted that such indiscretion and insensitivity could have happened within the highly secure premises where entry and exit is both highly controlled. It seems irrationality knowns no national boundaries.

August 28, 2016

□

NUCLEAR

27

Presence of Radioactivity in Steel could Dent the 'Make in India' Effort

Radioactively contaminated steel is a new cause for concern for manufacturing in India. An ironical steely paradox for Indian metal recyclers, on occasions steel products made in India are rejected at foreign ports of entry as they show up as a radiation hazard.

Recently, a shipment of utensils from India was confiscated at the Heathrow Airport in London as one of the packets exhibited high levels of radiation. This causes huge discomfiture for India's steel manufacturing sector and bad name for the country.

The Indian origin importer a UK-based restaurant owner is now running from pillar to post to avoid being penalized and battles an expensive litigation for what is really no fault of his. The original manufacturer of the utensils is currently untraceable. Obviously, a large batch of contaminated steel escaped scrutiny. Who knows where rest of the radioactively laced material is lying. Urgent steps are needed to trace rest of the missing utensils.

Since radiation has no smell, taste or colour and is hard to detect, any instance of radioactive leaks or contamination causes a huge scare. A false alarm of a radiological leak at the Indira Gandhi International Airport in New Delhi almost brought operations of the cargo terminal to a halt. Recently, the mere fear of the presence of radioactively contaminated gold left the government scurrying to contain damage in the high-end jewellery market.

Steel Recycling a Cause of Concern

The country's robust but un-organized steel re-cycling industry every so often runs into trouble as the finished products it makes are found to be contaminated with radioactive elements beyond the permissible limits. Some urgent measures are required to be put in place by the government curb this menace since in the business as usual approach the new 'Make in India' effort could take a beating in the long run.

Smt. Nirmala Sitharaman, Minister of State (Independent Charge) in the Ministry of Commerce & Industry recently told the Lok Sabha "in view of the risk to human life, property and national security, import of metal scrap in un-shredded compressed and loose form is permitted only through 26 designated ports" where portable scanners are being put in place. In addition pre-shipment certification is necessary to import scrap but then obviously some loop holes remain as contaminated steel continues to surface.

"A six-year study by the US Homeland Security showed that of the 123 shipments the Americans confiscated for radioactive contamination more than half had originated from India, highlighting that a lurking problem does exist needing to be tackled urgently. According to K.S. Parthasarathy, former Secretary of the Atomic Energy Regulatory Board (AERB), India's nuclear watchdog, radioactive contamination of steel products continues to be an issue in spite of massive efforts".

Just how does radioactivity creep into steel manufactured in the country? A common contaminant of steel is a radioactive element called Cobalt-60. It is widely used in the hi-tech industry as a radiation source for example in cancer treatment and in industrial applications like irradiating foods and for sterilizing surgical equipment. This radioactive element when it slips unnoticed into the steel making process, it leaves a trail that is hard to erase. According to the Department of Atomic Energy (DAE) most of the contaminations can be sourced to imported scrap metal, though domestic contamination can also not be ruled out fully.

AERB insists that India has a robust program to track all radioactive sources and hence chances of domestic contamination are minimal. However, the Mayapuri radiation incident of 2010 where a scrap dealer lost his life after the University of Delhi recklessly disposed of a Cobalt-60 machine blew the lid of this ticking time bomb. Until date, the scrap market of Mayapuri of Delhi remains unsafe as scant radiation monitoring takes place.

India is the third largest importer of steel scrap in the world next only to Turkey and South Korea; in 2013-14 the country imported about 5.7 million tonnes of steel scrap worth ₹ 30,456 crores. A 2015 estimate suggests that 60% of the Indian steel is produced using imported scrap. Subsequently, this recycled steel is largely exported back. This imported metal scrap occasionally comes in unnoticed contaminated with radioactive sources like Cobalt-60. This scrap when it is further melted and made into steel, the radioactivity gets dispersed even further.

Interestingly, in India imported scrap is still not fully scanned for radioactivity but on the contrary most Western nations have installed radioactivity detectors at ports of entry and hence seizure sat foreign ports are all too often. This is in spite of the fact that in the first place the radioactive contaminant substance may actually have originated from outside India.

A few years back Germany confiscated a whopping 150 tonnes of steel as it was contaminated with radioactive Cobalt-60. About a half of this was sent back to India and most of it seems lies locked up in Germany. France took action by removing electrical installations that were made in India as they showed a high level of radioactivity.

On the other hand, steel industry observers say Western nations use such punitive measures as non-tariff barriers to curb exports from India.

The Heathrow Scare

The contaminated steel bowl in question at Heathrow showed a radiation level of 80 micro Sievert per hour, which according to S. Hari Kumar, Secretary of the Atomic Energy Regulatory Board (AERB), Mumbai is an 'unacceptable' level. Nevertheless, was it dangerous? Parthasarathy says "my answer to the safe level of cobalt contamination is that no utensil with contamination is acceptable! If I know where they are, I shall remove them from use. What is the radiological impact of the steel utensil if it remains in circulation, though it is undesirable, I will not lose my sleep on the issue?" A logic hard to explain to the lay public.

The government through the AERB is trying to "intercept any case of radioactive material coming along with imports and steps are being taken to install sensitive radiation detectors at the major ports" says Hari Kumar. But the country still has a long way to go to ensure full compliance so that manufacturing in India does not take a hit due to avoidable contamination through orphan radioactive sources.

June 6, 2015

□

28

Waste to Wealth: BARC Pioneers New Life Saving Radiation Technology

Nobody really wants to mess with waste, let alone highly radioactive waste. Yet dirtying their hands Indian nuclear scientists for the first time in the world have harvested a rare form of a radioactive element called Caesium from the waste discarded from our atomic power plants.

Interestingly, this radioactive form of Caesium is then being deployed to sterilize blood to save lives and is also likely to find place in cleaning the River Ganga as part of the Swach Bharat Mission. Dr. Sekhar Basu, the new Chairman of Atomic Energy Commission confirmed "this technology is being used for the first time in the world in commercial domain."

Every ton of spent uranium nuclear fuel that emerges from India's atomic reactors produces about 500 litres of high-level waste that has to be handled with kid gloves in highly secure facilities and then disposed of using specialized glass containers.

This 500 litres of radioactive broth was earlier viewed as a waste for which money was spent on its disposal. However, earlier this year atomic engineers K. Banerjee and C.P. Kaushik working at the Bhabha Atomic Research

Centre (BARC) in Mumbai perfected a process by which high value elements like Caesium-137 could be safely harvested and then used for the benefit of humankind. Using some proprietary organic solvents, the chemists working at the Waste Immobilisation Plant in Trombay have managed to extract some useful products from this long-lived waste. In the new technology mastered by BARC, the Caesium-137 is impregnated into a glass medium and then made into what are called pencils these can then be used for as long as 30 years at a stretch. Like any other radiation source Caesium-137 pencils have to be kept shielded and handled only by trained personnel.

A few weeks ago, the first commercial consignment of ten pencils of Caesium-137 was handed over to medical authorities so that they could then be used to sterilize blood. This Caesium-137 has a special property of giving out certain radiations called Beta and Gamma rays that can be used to kill certain types of cells. In special medical conditions, safe blood transfusion can be done only when the White Blood Cells (WBCs) of the donor are killed off else fatal complications take place. In such cases, blood has to be irradiated and till now another chemical element Cobalt-60 was usually used. Kaushik says "the new Caesium based irradiator is more economical" and requires lesser handling so it is 'safer'.

This Caesium-137 can also be used for sterilizing sludge that is generated as a part of municipal waste. Earlier this year BARC inked a deal with the Ahmedabad Municipal Corporation to treat 100 tons of dry sewage sludge using a technique of safe irradiation using Cobalt-60. In the long run, Kaushik says Caesium-137 can also be used instead of Cobalt-60, which is not only costly to manufacture, and needs a highly specialized facility to make it. Today most of India's Cobalt-60 is manufactured at a special plant in Rawatbhata in Rajasthan.

Banerjee explains once larger quantities of Caesium-137 can be harvested, the same can then be used to clean the River Ganga as part of the National Mission to Clean the Ganga or 'Namami Gange Project' that hopes to give back to India an 'aviral and nirmal Ganga'. Today the bacterial load in the river is very high at places approaching over million times more than the permissible level. These harmful bacteria can be effectively killed off if the sewage is treated with nuclear radiation. The process has been found to be safe and the treated municipal waste can then be safely used as fertilizer without the fear of dangerous infections being contracted.

Sewage treatment using radiation is not new to India. According to Dr. Jitendra Singh, Minister of State in the Prime Minister's Office looking after the activities of the Department of Atomic Energy recently noted that the "Bhabha Atomic Research Centre has developed the technology for sewage sludge hygienisation using Gamma Radiation. A demonstration plant, Sludge Hygienisation Research Irradiator (SHRI) has been jointly set up at Vadodara in Gujarat by BARC, Vadodara Municipal Corporation and Government of Gujarat and has been in operation for about sixteen years. In the process, wet sludge containing about 4% solid and 96% water is hygienised using radiation. This wet sludge is poured into drying beds where under sunlight the wet sludge dries to solid cake. This hygienised solid cake is used in agricultural practices. It has been observed that directly hygienising solid cake is more economical and scalable to meet the requirement of big towns and cities. The technology can be used in cities and towns where sewage treatment plants exist."

The same newly made Caesium-137 can also be used to give onions a longer shelf life. Every now and then prices of onion shoot up and occasionally governments get destabilized due to rising prices of onion. The Board of Radiation and Isotope Technology (BRIT) already operates plants in Maharashtra that use radiation to increase the shelf life of onions and potatoes. Today these plants use Cobalt-60, tomorrow the radiation source can be Caesium-137 explains Banerjee.

The global nuclear watchdog, the International Atomic Energy Agency (IAEA) has lauded this breakthrough from BARC and promises to popularise it. Banerjee said he was recently in China, which also appreciated the development. A remarkable Indian contribution for generating wealth from waste while contributing to the Swach Bharat Mission.

October 25, 2015

□

29

Kakrapar Atomic Plant Leak Exposes a 'Mysterious' Chink in Armour; Indian Nuclear Plants Need Urgent Systemic Safety Review

The nuclear leak at the Kakrapar Atomic Power Station (KAPS) continues unabated more than a week later at the indigenously made 220-megawatt nuclear reactor in southern Gujarat. Despite best efforts, it continues to leak a mixture of light and heavy water. The exact cause of the leak also remains a mystery. India has another 17 reactors of the same Pressurized Heavy Water Reactor (PHWR) type that continue to operate and the big question is, should the entire fleet be grounded until the mystery of the leak is fully resolved?

The Kakrapar Unit-1 reactor was running at best capacity when the first leakage of steam was detected visually on remotely operated cameras on the morning of March 11, 2016, later as pressure rose in the huge double contained reactor building a plant emergency was immediately declared. Subsequently, all safety systems worked with precision bringing the nuclear chain reaction to a halt. The 350 workers at the plant remained safe as none was stationed in the area where the leak took place. Sekhar

Basu, Chairman of the Atomic Energy Commission, Mumbai said "a feeder piper carrying heavy water leaked and all radioactivity was confined within the reactor building itself and no radiation escaped outside the plant".

A week later the plant though remains in a 'safe shutdown condition' 'yet the accident that occurred at 9 am on March 11 is a wake-up call on the safety of Indian power plants. Now top experts and not just anti-nuclear activists are calling for an overall review of the safety of the 21 nuclear power plants of the country that can together generate 5780 MW of power, and also give India its huge nuclear weapons punch.

According to the Indian nuclear watchdog, the Atomic Energy Regulatory Board (AERB), no plant worker has been exposed to radioactivity and nor has any radioactivity been released into the environment. AERB reports that "a small part of the cooling water is continuing to leak out of the coolant system". It seems the venting of built -up pressure did not release any radiation as the experts from the Environmental Safety Laboratory of the Bhabha Atomic Research Centre did not find any increased levels of radiation or radioactive contamination in a 20 km radius of the plant.

Workers wearing special radiation safety suits have entered the reactor building but plugging the leak will take longer and according to AERB "investigations could take considerable time".

The timing of the accident could not have been worse, it happened by the date on the fifth anniversary of the serial meltdown of atomic power plants at Fukushima in Japan. The Kakrapar leak was a "serious incident and a big surprise" says Shiv Abhilash Bhardwaj, Chairman of the AERB and no-nonsense veteran nuclear engineer, who says "a leak of this nature in an actively running atomic station has never occurred in India".

There was "no inkling for such an incident especially from such a young reactor" explained Bhardwaj. Even though the reactor is about 24 years old, according to AERB "the pressure tubes of the coolant channels in this reactor were replaced with new ones made from improved material in the year 2011, as part of pressure tube aging management programme". Experts are surprised that special Zircaloy tubes failed so soon after being changed. The usual life of a reactor varies from 40-60 years. India's oldest reactors at Tarapur in Maharashtra have been running for almost 47 years.

"This leak should not have taken place", explains Anil Kakodkar, former Chairman of the Atomic Energy Commission, Mumbai, "there is no doubt that first level of safety was unfortunately breached but subsequently all other backup systems kicked in as designed" says Kakodkar. "There was a failure of the in-service inspection mechanism and lessons need to be learnt" says Kakodkar who has spent nearly 40 years working with Indian reactors. He says the need is to learn "how to avert re-occurrence of such an incident" towards that Kakodkar calls for a "systemic review to ensure such failures reach near zero levels".

Reactors were Stress Tested

After the catastrophic nuclear accident at Fukushima, almost all nuclear reactors of the world underwent 'stress tests' to ensure they can withstand accidents of that nature. Indian reactors were also subjected to an extensive review under the leadership of Dr. S.K. Sharma a former head of AERB. Yet, within four years after having been thoroughly examined a "breakage or leakage in the robust primary coolant system at Kakrapar", has taken many experts aback.

India has until date accumulated about 410 reactor years of experience. This Kakrapar accident which in the complicated mumbo-jumbo of nuclear engineers is still classed as 'an incident' is considered the second worst mishap in India's more than half a century of nuclear experience. Nuclear experts still quake in their feet when they recall the 1993 fire incident at the Narora Atomic Power Station in Uttar Pradesh, where a near meltdown was narrowly averted simply because the alert Indian nuclear engineers acted boldly and bravely. The Kakrapar accident though is more worrying since it happened on the secure nuclear island of an operating atomic reactor whose performance has been exemplary.

At the time of the accident, the reactor was loaded with about 100 tonnes of natural uranium and an unknown quantity of heavy water leaked in the first 24-36 hours after the accident. However, when officials finally entered the double contained vaulted part of the plant according to Bhardwaj his team reported back to him that the place was 'spic and span' suggesting that the leak was 'small' as the Site Director of the Kakrapar Atomic Power Station L.K. Jain had reported on the day of the leak. Basu says inherently the design of the PHWR is one of the safest in the world and a large-scale accident of the type that happened at Chernobyl in 1986 is highly unlikely.

To give some credit to the Indian nuclear establishment not a single human life has been lost due to radiation exposure at the government's atomic energy facilities. The only death directly attributable to radiation exposure in the country took place due to the utter carelessness of learned professors of the Chemistry Department at the University of Delhi in 2010 when they dumped a Cobalt-60 radioactive source and an un-suspecting scarp dealer lost his life.

According to estimates by the World Nuclear Association, "India has a flourishing and largely indigenous nuclear power programme and expects to have 14,600 MW nuclear capacity on line by 2024 and 63 GW by 2032. It aims to supply 25% of electricity from nuclear power by 2050." Towards this Finance Minister Arun Jailtley in his 2016 budget speech said "government is drawing up a comprehensive plan, spanning next 15 to 20 years, to augment the investment in nuclear power generation." Budgetary allocation up to ₹ 3,000 crore per annum, together with public sector investments, will be leveraged to facilitate the required investment for this purpose. But to be able to achieve such lofty goals the Indian nuclear establishment will have to work extra hard to win the hearts and minds of the Indian public to ensure that confidence is not lost in the promise of nuclear power a much needed carbon-free source of energy in times of a changing climate. The government also needs to make sure that the Nuclear Safety Regulatory Authority Bill is passed post haste in the Parliament.

According to AERB, "a detailed plan for isolating the leak [from Kakrapar plant] was submitted by the Nuclear Power Corporation of India Limited (NPCIL) and it has reviewed the plan in detail and given clearance for going ahead with its implementation with necessary precautions". Bhardwaj confirms that until the exact cause of the leakage is not pinpointed and till AERB is convinced whether the 'failure is specific to the Kakrapar atomic reactor or is it a generic problem all caution has to be exercised'. Bhardwaj says as of now he is not ordering an all-out shutdown of Indian heavy water atomic reactors simply because the back-up safety systems worked 'perfectly' at Kakrapar. In the meanwhile, the Kakrapar plant "has been asked to remain in safe shutdown state till the investigations and corrective actions are completed". A wake-up call for the Indian nuclear industry that hopes to increase its nuclear capacity by 12 times in the next 16 years. "We need to do a root cause analysis" says Kakodkar.

March 20, 2016

□

30

Fourteen Year 'Vanvas' Ends in Kudankulam Bringing Cheers & Tears at India's Secretive Nuclear Establishment

At India's highly guarded and walled atomic establishment cheers in southern India and tears in western India!

Much to cheer about at Kudankulam, here India's largest nuclear power park situated not far from the tip of India Kanyakumari is now operational. The twin 1000 MW atomic reactors have the nuclear fission reaction running in them for the first time. The first unit started supplying electricity in 2013 and the second unit which became operational this week and will start feeding electricity to the grid in a few weeks.

At the same time, some 2000 kilometres away some grief and tears since the indigenously made Kakrapar Atomic Power Station in Gujarat remains shut for nearly four months after a leak in the nuclear island of the reactor forced an emergency shutdown of a fully operating plant. The bigger headache for the Indian nuclear engineers is that even after several months of investigation the exact reason why the 'leak' took place remains a mystery. The usually mild mannered but vigilant nuclear watchdog of India the Atomic Energy Regulatory Board (AERB) issued an ominous statement which said "the incident of leak from a coolant channel at Kakrapar Atomic Power Station Unit 1 at an early stage of its life has raised some concerns".

At Kudankulam which is not far from Lanka the 14 year hiatus in starting the atomic reactors is almost akin to the 14 year *'vanvas'* or banishment for Lord Rama as recorded in the religious epic *Ramayana*. The nuclear *'vanvas'* for Kudankulam ended on July 10, 2016 when the first sustained nuclear fission was attained in the second unit of the Russian made nuclear reactors. The construction for the first two units began way back in 2002 with the target to make it operational in five years, but today it has taken almost three times that amount of time. Time overruns on infrastructure projects prove to be very costly especially since Tamil Nadu was woefully short of electricity.

The large reactors at Kudankulam have been delayed for various reasons, there was considerable delay in supplying parts by Russian manufacturers and then just as the first unit was to become operational three years ago an anti-nuclear agitation in part initially fuelled by the local State Government of Tamil Nadu halted work at the almost ready atomic plants.

Today the two atomic reactors at Kudankulam have cost over ₹ 22,000 crores confirms S.K. Sharma the Chairman-cum-Managing Director of the Nuclear Power Corporation of India Limited (NPCIL) the operator of the plant. The ten year delay escalated the cost of the reactors by almost ₹ 9000 crores. A huge drain on the exchequer.

Local anti-nuclear activists like S.P. Udayakumar dub the reactors as 'unsafe' and call them a huge risk for the people living around the giant reactors. The fairly affluent fisher folk who inhabit the village closet to the nuclear reactors called Idinthakarai erupted against the establishment of the atomic reactors in their backyard and forced the plant authorities to delay the start of the reactors. Countering the claims of the activists, the then Chairman of the Atomic Energy Commission Dr. Srikumar Banerjee had called the Kudankulam reactors 'one of the safest in the world'.

In fact, on the day both the reactors became operational NPCIL issued a statement saying the Russian-made reactors are what are called Generation three plus atomic power plants, calling them 'state-of-the-art' reactors that incorporate enhanced safety features ensuring the highest level of safety, in line with the current international standards. These have a combination of active safety systems as well as passive safety systems like passive heat removal system, hydrogen recombiners, core catcher, hydro accumulators and quick boron injection system. This combination of multi-layered safety features ensures safety of the plant, public and environment.

It was a combination of failures in outreach that seems to have fuelled the anti-nuclear agitation around the Kudankulam reactors. The plant authorities admitted that they failed to reach the village of Idinthakarai to convince them about the safety features of the plant. In addition just as the first unit of the Kudankulam plant was getting ready in 2011 the nuclear accident at Fukushima in Japan shook the world and left the largely Christian fishing community around Kudankulam in a heightened state of fear.

To add fuel to the fire around the same time period, NPCIL conducted a crucial test of a pressure relief valve for the giant reactor which can likened to ultra-big pressure cooker in the middle of the night. This involved dumping steam from the 1000 MW reactor and the noise it made was heard as far away as 20 kilometres from the reactors. Imagine the ruckus a tiny pressure cooker makes in the kitchen and everyone in the neighbourhood knows something is cooking, multiply this millions of times and that was the sound that shocked and rocked the residents. No advance warning was issued and when it happened locals feared that like the explosions at Fukushima the atomic reactors at Kudankulam had exploded. Nothing of that sort had happened and it was only a controlled experiment that went wrong in outreach. This agitation brought the all-powerful Department of Atomic Energy the fountainhead of India's nuclear weapons down on to its knees.

It was really the fear of the unknown that fuelled the anti-nuclear agitation since invariably atomic plants are hidden behind high walls and guarded by armed forces. For some bizarre reason nuclear engineers tend to work at their best efficiency at night. Having created such a scare in the minds of the locals by their midnight test of the pressure valve, the criticality or the start of the nuclear fission reaction for both units 1 and 2 was triggered in darkness when the fear factor is always higher. The latest milestone for unit 2 was reached at 8.56 pm on Sunday last. It seems by now the locals had developed some trust since no protests erupted in the aftermath. Locals seem to have learnt a lasting lesson, but for some reason the Indian atomic establishment continues to live like an ostrich not internalizing a simple fact key milestones should preferably be undertaken during daylight hours.

If India has to establish 63,000 MW of nuclear plants by 2032 as is the government's plan then winning the hearts and minds of people living around atomic reactors has be undertaken at a warfooting. There is a suggestion that the AERB should make it mandatory that locals be sensitized on crucial tests and that such events should be undertaken only during daylight hours.

In a few weeks, the Kudankulam plant will start generating full 2000 MW of power helping the states of Tamil Nadu, Kerala, Karnataka and Puducherry bridge the power shortage. India now houses 22 reactors with a total installed capacity of 6780 MW.

Now the tears:

The 220 MW Indian made nuclear reactor located at Kakrapar in southern Gujarat failed on the morning of March 11, 2016. A leak developed and the automatic systems brought the reactor to a halt as AERB asserts "there was no hazard to the operators and the public". No radioactivity leaked out beyond permissible levels and no one suffered any radiation sickness.

Yet four months after 'incident', the exact cause of the leak has not been deciphered according to AERB preliminary investigation have revealed that "the failed coolant channel is seen to have three cracks...the leaky coolant channel is yet to be removed from the reactor for detailed failure analysis and establishing the causes. Preparatory work for the removal of the channel from the reactor is currently in progress. Removal of this failed channel requires careful planning and preparedness as vital information on nature and causes of failure is not lost during the removal".

Why should this single failed coolant channel worry India? India currently operates 17 similar reactors of the type that developed a leak at Kakrapar and together according to AERB that would number some 5000 coolant channels. At this moment, it is hazardous to guess how the other coolant channels are faring? According to AERB, as an immediate measure the sensitive leak detection systems installed at all operating atomic stations has been 'rechecked' by NPCIL.

Yet the AERB raises a red flag when it says "during the ongoing inspections at Kakrapar units, unusual indications of local corrosion spots was noticed on the coolant channels, ...AERB asked for inspection of coolant channels of other units to rule out the possibility of similar corrosion." After a suitable review, the AERB suggests that "the presence of local corrosion spots is specific to Kakrapar units alone and no evidence of this phenomenon is seen in other reactors inspected so far". This is indeed worrying and the sooner

NPCIL completes these inspections the better it will be for India's ambitious nuclear program. "Not mincing words the AERB says exact reasons for the failure of Kakrapar Atomic Power Station Unit 1 can be established after completion of the failure analysis, which is expected to take considerable time".

The redeeming fact is that in the over 40 years of combined reactor operating experience that India has accumulated while running 22 reactors since 1969 not a single death has occurred due to radiation exposure at India's nuclear power plants. Hopefully, this record will remain unblemished.

Even as nuclear engineers cheer and celebrate the first full operation of India's largest nuclear power park at Kudankulam on nine other sites which house atomic reactors atomic scientists spend sleepless nights checking the reliability of systems to avoid any mishaps. Only nuclear sweat can wipe the tears to once again bring cheers at all Indian atomic units. Meanwhile southern India eagerly awaits newly generated 'atomic electricity' with bated breath.

July 17, 2016

□

31

At Pokharan, Indian designed planes & missiles show firepower. DRDO quietly exults

In the deserts of Pokharan, not far from the border with Pakistan, the Indian Air Force (IAF) displayed its might. In less than four hours, 181 aeroplanes bombed several targets. For the very first time in India's history, indigenously made potent missiles like Akash and Astra were openly fired in front of a discerning audience. This exercise called 'Iron Fist 2016' also showcased the firing potential of country's highly versatile Tejas fighter aircraft or the Light Combat Aircraft (LCA). Sources in the Defence Research and Development Organisation (DRDO) confirmed that this was the first time India's Prime Minister and President of India were witnessing in front of their eyes the immense capability of these Indian made weapon platforms.

The DRDO, once dubbed as the 'Defenceless Research and Dud Organisation', quietly celebrated the debut firing of its lead platforms in an open 'operational fire power demonstration' that was also beamed live all over the world and in front of defence attaches of the most powerful countries of the world.

India's multi-role fighter jet, Tejas showed its prowess by performing twin roles in the same sortie. The 9800-kilogram supersonic plane first came and from high above the witnessing stand, fired a laser-guided bomb onto a target on the ground. Then it converted itself from a ground attack platform into an air-to-air combat mean machine. In the same flight, the LCA fired a missile onto an aerial target. Technically, it fired an R-73E missile onto a simulated enemy plane.

The graceful LCA, mostly designed in Bengaluru, executed its roles with elegance, but subsequently there were reports that the bomb dropped by Tejas missed its target possibly because the fuse of the bomb miss-performed and to the naked eye, it also seemed that the air-to-air missile fired by the LCA did not directly hit the 'flare' which was being used as simulated enemy war-plane. Though later, it was clarified that the R-73E missile did hit the target but since the flare is 'miniscule' compared to full-fledged enemy air plane, it may have seemed to have gone awry. Any which ways, the Indian plane that costs about ₹ 200 crores a piece or about $ 28 million is a unique fighting machine. In comparison, the Rafale Jet costs upwards of ₹ 1600 crores a piece.

Much has been written that the first sanction for the design of the LCA started in 1983 and by now, as per a report by the Comptroller and Auditor General of India, the Ministry of Defence has invested ₹ 10,397 crores on this project. Despite this long gestation, the plane is considered the best in its class with the IAF hopefully going to induct these planes into the battle-ready cadre this year. The IAF is already short of nine squadrons of fighter planes.

To some of the naysayers of Tejas, a fact should be driven that it does take anywhere between 15 years and 20 years to design a new fighter plane even by advanced countries that have serially produced fighter jets. For India, this was really only a second venture albeit with a huge gap.

Recently, the Tejas also had its first foreign debut when earlier this year when two planes flew to perform aerobatics at the Bahrain International Air Show essentially India expressing its desire that this 'Made in India' plane could be exported if required by other countries.

Now well-meaning and knowledgeable defence experts are even questioning whether India really needs to go ahead and buy either 36 or the 126 'Medium Multi-Role Combat Aircraft' like the Rafale at all. The first 'request for proposal' was put out almost 15 years ago and till date, the Indian Air Force and the Indian government have not really made up their minds on how to cross the last mile for this purchase. Now that the LCA is almost near, the finish line it possibly makes sense to opt for an Indian made plane rather than depend on an expensive foreign vendor, even though the LCA comes with a third of the payload-carrying capacity and a third of the range. Many in the IAF who decry the delays in the making of the Tejas should also answer with parity the delays in simply buying off the shelf foreign fighter planes. If the need was so pressing to bridge, the gap for replacing the aging Mig-21s, then why is the IAF and the government not able to make a decision for the last 15 years. Maybe now that both President Pranab Mukherjee and Prime Minister Narendra Modi have personally seen the Tejas platform fire ammunition last week, an afterthought may occur and the local effort could just zoom past.

The DRDO also highlighted its ASTRA missile, a beyond visual range air-to-air missile capable of engaging targets from anywhere between 20 and 80 kilometres. This missile was fired from a Sukhoi-30 MKI aircraft and sources said it hit the target, but since it goes and strikes a target beyond the visual range, there was no possibility of witnessing the hit. This was the first time the DRDO publicly showed its advanced air-to-air missile, which is capable of undertaking as claimed some manoeuvres at 40 G levels making it very versatile. This 3.8-metre length missile has been under development for ten years.

At Pokharan, in a night, firing the IAF for the first time highlighted its recent indigenous acquisition, the Akash Missile System. A single missile was fired from very close to place where the VIP stand and it left behind a smoke trail before disappearing after the imaginary enemy target in the night sky. According to DRDO, which developed the Akash missile system, it is a 'medium-range surface-to-air missile with multi-target engagement capability. It uses high-energy solid propellant for the booster and ram-rocket propulsion for the main phase. The propulsion system provides higher level of energy with minimum mass, compared to conventional solid/liquid rocket motor that has better performance with minimum weight of the missile. It has a dual mode guidance, initially on command mode from a phased array radar and, later, radar homing guidance with unique software developed for high accuracy. The phased array radar provides capability for multiple target tracking and simultaneous deployment of missiles to attack four targets, at the same time, in each battery. Multiple batteries constitute a group centre. The system is highly mobile.' India has already developed under its Integrated Guided Missile Development Program missile like Prithvi, Agni, Trishul and Akash. Until date, only Akash has been fired in the presence of top dignitaries and as one DRDO official put, 'it shows the high level of confidence the IAF is putting in the Akash missile system'. The IAF has already ordered eight squadrons of the Akash missile system at a cost of over ₹ 23,000 crores and reports suggest that the system has already been deployed in Jorhat, Gwalior, Tejpur, Hashimara and Pune. It is estimated that DRDO spent close to ₹ 1000 crore in the R&D of this missile system. A comparable foreign system would be ten times more costly to purchase than the Indian made system.

According to estimates by the DRDO, thanks to its contribution India's defence R&D today, the country is just one of the five countries to have its own ballistic missile defence program; one of the six countries to have developed a nuclear-powered submarine; one of the seven countries to have developed its own main battle tank and an indigenous 4th-gen combat aircraft. The production value of systems based on DRDO technologies that have been inducted and or approved for induction into services during the past decade (excluding strategic systems) stands at over ₹ 1,70,000 crores.

It is not easy to do research and development of high-grade weapon systems and DRDO says often it is unfairly targeted of its delays and inefficiencies when actually the acquisitions lobby tries to scuttle local development. This showcasing of the missile systems and the Tejas plane at Pokharan in a way suggests the coming of age of the 'Made in India' platforms even as lobbies push for the 'Make in India' effort. The difference is subtle but the implications huge especially in times of war.

March 27, 2016

□

PERSONALITY

32

'Kalam Island' should be the New Name of Wheeler Island, the '*Karam Bhoomi*' of India's Missile Man A.P.J. Abdul Kalam

There is a growing demand that as a fitting tribute to former President A.P.J. Abdul Kalam, the country's most advanced missile testing site in the Bay of Bengal should now be named 'Kalam Island'. It was here that Kalam tested scores of missiles. The quiet sea washed sylvan surroundings also gave him inspiration to write many poems for his book *My Journey*.

India's missile man aeronautical engineer *par excellence* Kalam took his last flight into the heavens to find place among stars on July 28, 2015, it is time his most loved playground a tiny island off the Odisha coast be named in his memory as 'Kalam Island'. As the man pioneering missile development in India, he himself described the Wheeler Island as his 'theatre of action'. The first successful land-to-land test of the Prithvi Missile was conducted from the mainland and it landed on the then uninhabited 'Wheeler Island' on November 30, 1993.

Having travelled to the Wheeler Island many times, I am aware of how the island itself is steeped in history of the successes and failures encountered during the missile development program and the whole place is replete with tales about Kalam's escapades. Ironically, the island is today named after an English commandant Lieutenant Wheeler.

"It is high time we need to call it Kalam Island since it is a one of its kind hi-tech facility in India and it was actually spotted and built from scratch by Kalam" asserts V.K. Saraswat Member of the National Institution for Transforming India (NITI Aayog), New Delhi. Saraswat was Kalam's associate for 35 years as a missile scientist and then rose to be the Director General of the Defence Research and Development Organisation (DRDO). In 1993, it was Saraswat and his co-worker S.K. Salwan who as scientists were the first to set foot on the 'Wheeler Island' when Kalam instructed them to look for these uninhabited islands that he had initially spotted on the naval hydrographic maps.

Saraswat recalls that sultry day in 1993 when he hired a boat for ₹ 250 and then got lost in the Bay of Bengal and had to spend the night on the Wheeler Island itself surviving on bananas. The islands were not visible from the mainland. Recalling of this incident by writing in his 2014 book *Ignited Minds: Unleashing the Power Within India"* Kalam writes "to their surprise they [Saraswat and Salwan] found a Bangladeshi flag flying atop a tree, as the island may have been frequented by fishermen from the neighbouring country. My friends quickly removed the flag". S.K. Salwan recalls that over the years, Kalam may have visited the Wheeler Island more than dozen times and hence this was truly his 'playground'.

The 'Wheeler Island' is also home to famous Olive Riddley Turtles who come in hordes to nest on its sandy beaches. Legend goes that it was Kalam who was responsible to ensure that lights on the island were dimmed to ensure that the baby turtles do not get lost by getting attracted to artificial lights and missile testing was restrained during the turtle-nesting season.

In a talk to civil servants in 2012, Kalam himself recalled the process of the discovery of the Wheeler Islands "when we were progressing the missile programme and Prithvi had demonstrated successful performance, Army came up with another important requirement. Army desired to have a confirmatory test, on a land range, to validate Circular Error Probability (CEP). Our efforts to conduct the tests in our desert range could not take off due to range safety and geopolitical problems. To overcome this we were looking for an uninhabited island in the Eastern coast. On the hydrographic map supplied by Navy, we saw a few islands in the Bay of Bengal off Dhamra (Orissa coast) indicating that there was some landmass. Our range team consisting of Dr. S.K. Salwan and Dr. V.K. Saraswat hired a boat from Dhamra and went in search of the island. On the map these islands were marked as 'long wheeler', 'coconut wheeler' and 'small wheeler'. The team carried a directional compass and proceeded on the journey. They lost their way and could not locate the Wheeler Island. Fortunately, they met few fishing boats and asked them for the route. The fisherman did not know about the Wheeler Island but they said there was an Island called 'Chandrachood'. They thought that this could be the Wheeler Island. They approximately gave the direction for proceeding to Chandrachood. With this help the team could reach the Chandrachood Island, which was later confirmed as Small Wheeler Island which had adequate width and length required for range operations. For getting the island, we went through the Odisha bureaucracy and at a particular point of time, we had to seek a political decision from the Chief Minister in (1993). At that time a powerful national leader Biju Patnaik was the Chief Minister. The indications from the Chief Minister's office were that the island cannot be parted with due to several reasons. However, an appointment was arranged for meeting the Chief Minister and put my request. When we reached his office, the file was in front of him. Chief Minister Biju Patnaikji said, Kalam, I have decided to give all the five islands at no cost to you (DRDO), but I will sign the file of approval only when you give me a promise. Chief Minister held my hand and said, I have an invitation to visit China. I will visit only when you promise that you will make a missile that will reach China. I said, Chief Minister Sir, definitely, we will work for it. I immediately informed our Defence Minister. Chief Minister signed the file and I got the island, particularly the small wheeler island."

Incidentally, it was Kalam's protégée Saraswat who nine years later used the same island to successfully launch Agni 5, the country's long range missile that could target China fulfilling Biju Patnaik's request.

Today the 'Wheeler Island' has seen about 75 different tests of missiles from the short range Prithvi missile to India's maiden inter continental ballistic missile Agni-5 that has range of over 5000 kilometres all being flown from Kalam's 'theatre of action'. There is even a granite memorial called 'Prithvi Point' which was the original impact point for that crucial 1993 test after which the Indian armed forces decided to induct the missile in their arsenal. All three service Chiefs witnessed the landmark test. Salwan recalls the entire Island was on fire after the strike, which had hit bull's eye.

The group of three islands a few square kilometres in area are located some 10 kilometres from the mainland and are today one of the most heavily guarded facilities of the Ministry of Defence. It can be approached only by a boat and no civilian resides on it but is replete with high tech facilities to launch, track and monitor launch of ballistic missiles.

In times to come, Wheeler Island by then hopefully renamed could well witness the launch of more advanced "missiles. Sudhir Mishra, CEO and Managing Director of

BrahMos Aerospace Limited recalls of his last meeting with Kalam where he mandated BrahMos Aerospace to build a 'missile system that would be hypersonic, very long range, re-usable, capable of carrying a strategic payload and that it should very-very cost-effective." Mishra promises to fulfil Kalam's dream.

Salwan recalls Kalam so well-known for his humaneness always thought about the welfare of locals and the Wheeler Island was made a missile testing range essentially to ensure that locals were not inconvenienced because of the mandatory evacuation that was done at the Balasore test site on the mainland whenever a big missile was tested. According to Salwan, "it was Kalam's dream to develop a safe missile range and the shifting sands of the island were converted into a launch pad in two years". Salwan fondly recalls that Kalam used reiterate "let me leave my footprints on the sand of time and not printed on stones".

Saraswat says the 'Wheeler Island' is the world best site to launch missiles and by renaming the island as 'Kalam Island' it could be 'a small token of remembrance', for a man who made India proud on many fronts and dreamt of a time when India would be a developed country.

Prime Minister Narendra Modi called Kalam as his '*margdarshak*' so after his final flight the time has come to etch his name in gold for eternity by renaming his 'theatre of action' as Kalam Island an institution of modern science he built from scratch for the safety and security of the common man of the country. This would be a new beginning for the country's 'peoples president' as Kalam himself wrote 'End is not the end, END means Effort Never Dies!'

August 2, 2015

□

33

Mother Teresa was a Living 'God' Why Attribute Irrational Miracles to Her for Granting Her the Status of a Saint

In her life time, she had already earned the title 'saint of the gutters' and to the thousands of destitute and needy who she cared for she was a 'living God'. Now today Agnes Gonxha Bojakhiu (87) a catholic nun who served the poor in Kolkata will be formally bestowed the title of Saint Teresa by Pope John Paul II in a function at the Vatican City.

Her journey from her birthplace Skopje now in Macedonia to her yeoman work in West Bengal is itself a 'miracle' but after her death to attribute this diminutive woman with a Herculean grit for serving the poor of having performed 'miracles' like curing two people of diseases borders on irrationality. Mother Teresa should have been made a saint without having so-called miracles associated with her name.

It is worth highlighting that the Constitution of India in Article 51A(h) enunciates "to develop the scientific temper, humanism and the spirit of inquiry and reform". This is where attribution of so-called miracles comes into conflict with the understandings of modern science. But India is complex civilisation where faith, science, religion and superstition all coexist mostly in harmony but occasionally in conflict.

India's best known living scientist and recent Bharat Ratna Professor C.N.R. Rao on being asked said. "No, I do not believe in miracles. One thing in general I will tell you, in India there is confusion between religion, faith, superstition and science. Faith everybody should have one thing or the other, like if in science you must have faith in the laws of physics. Faith is something everybody should have. If somebody has faith in philosophy or God, I have nothing against it; however, it should not give rise to superstition. Even Einstein said nobody could be without faith. Religion also you can have any religion, but do not mix it up with other things in life. Faith has nothing to do with believing in things that cannot happen against the laws of physics."

But for Mother Teresa to officially become a saint she needed to perform some miracles and according to the National Catholic Register, "The first [miracle] took place in West Bengal, India, and involved the healing of an Indian woman, Monica Besra, whose abdominal tumour was so severe that her doctors abandoned hope of saving her. Taken into the care of the Missionaries of Charity, she continued to decline and endured such agony from the tumour that she could no longer sleep. On the one-year anniversary of Mother's passing, the sisters at the home placed a Miraculous Medal that had been touched to the body of Mother Teresa on Besra's stomach. The suffering woman fell asleep, and when she woke up, her pain was gone. Doctors examined her and found the reason why: The tumour had disappeared completely."

"Busting some of the hype around the miracle in 2003 *The New York Times* reported quoting Dr. Ranjan Mustafi, a doctor who said he had treated Besra, and claimed that "the medicines he prescribed had eliminated the tumour." He also said it was a cyst caused by tuberculosis, not a cancerous tumour. The Vatican team that travelled to India and certified Ms. Besra's account, he added, never made contact with him."

According to the National Catholic Register, "A board of medical specialists worked with the Congregation for the Causes of Saints to study the alleged miracle. After assessing the records and interviewing the medical staff involved, the committee determined that the healing was medically inexplicable." Pope John Paul approved the miracle on December 20, 2002, barely five years after Teresa's death. "But speaking to the *New York Times* in 2003 Besra's physician said "It was not a miracle," Mustafi said. "She took medicines for nine months to one year."

According to the National Catholic Register, "the second miracle took place in December 2008 in Brazil. Marcilio Haddad Andrino, a now-42-year-old mechanical engineer from Santos, Brazil, struggled with a bacterial infection in the brain that caused severe brain abscesses and agonizing head pain. A priest friend encouraged the recently married young man and his wife, Fernanda Nascimento Rocha, to pray for Mother Teresa's help. Andrino, however, slipped into a coma as treatments failed, and while Rocha prayed, he was taken in for last-ditch surgery. When the surgeon entered the operating room, he found Andrino awake and asking him what was going on. Andrino made a full recovery, and the couple went on to have two children, even though it was deemed by doctors to be a near medical impossibility."

Rationalists oppose tooth and nail that miracles take place since most so-called miracles have a scientific basis. Take the case of 1995 rumour that statues of Lord Ganesha were drinking milk, devotees lined up in thousands outside temples offering milk to the elephant God. In the end, it turned out that simple laws of physics and how a meniscus behaves could well explain why milk was disappearing from a spoon and heading down towards mother earth due to laws of gravity. Yet to date you can see gullible people being taken in by *fakirs, babas* and priests for performing miracles. One common miracle is exorcism of a ghost from person body using a coconut and by sprinkling water on the coconut. In reality, the miracle maker usually hides a piece of sodium metal within the husk of the coconut and when water is sprinkled on it, the sodium catches fire gives out a smoke and the people are fooled into believing that the ghost was cleansed from the victim's body. In reality, it was a heat giving or exothermic reaction of water and sodium that became a ghost excommunicated.

Similarly, the two miraculous medical recoveries attributed to Mother Teresa would have a rational medical explanation but to the believers faith over powers science. It is high time the Catholic Church gave up this requirement of a person having performed at least two miracles after death to be canonized into saint hood. Reform seems to be taking place in the church since earlier there was a requirement of more miracles to have been recorded and there was a mandatory fifty year waiting period for a person to be declared a saint, but in Mother Teresa's case that has been waived and she would be officially granted sainthood within two decades after her death. This is indeed a miracle by the conservative church.

Most Indians will be celebrating the elevation of Saint Teresa and India's Minister for External Affairs Sushma Swaraj will represent the might of the Indian Constitution at the August Ceremony yet there are a few who question the rationality of such exercises. Speaking on this issues, Prabir Ghosh, President of the Science and Rationalists Association of India from Kolkata said "if people want to revere Mother Teresa for her social work, I have no problem. But these miracles are unreasonable. I challenge the Pope to cure every poor person in India who cannot afford medical care, by praying to Mother Teresa".

On the other hand, Rao is also fellow of the Pontifical Academy of Sciences, and on being asked about this issue of Mother Teresa being made into a Saint and how does he justify miracles and science? Rao points out that "Pontifical Academy has nothing to do with the Pope in this way, Pope deals with the church and the church has made her a saint. Pontifical Academy does not deal with Saints." Towards lasting peace Rao has simple solution "do not mix religion and science".

According to an official release from the Popes Office in her own life time Mother Teresa said "what the poor need most is to feel needed, to feel loved. There are remedies and treatments for all kinds of illnesses, but when someone is undesirable, if there are no serving hands and loving hearts, then there is no hope for a true cure."

It is for these reasons attributing scientifically unproven remedies as miracles does not help the followers of Missionaries of Charity and humanity in general. For the thousands of destitute that Mother Teresa treated she was 'God incarnate' and her hand was the miracle of love the poor needed.

September 4, 2016

□

34

M.G.K. Menon a Remarkable Polymath Scientist Leaves a Behind Big Void!

A living legend M.G.K. Menon passed away this week, a very unique Indian scientist who made huge contributions in almost equal measure in fields as diverse as high energy physics, electronics, atomic energy, space, environment and biotechnology has left to make the next world an even better place.

It is rare to find scientists who are also great institution builders, Professor Mambillikalathil Govind Kumar Menon, or MGK to most and 'Goku' to his friends was one such rare personality. At the age of 88, Menon passed away leaving a legacy that is well remembered.

Menon is recognized for his work on high energy physics especially his work on cosmic rays, muons and atmospheric neutrinos. A gentle man to the core whose impeccable command over English and no-nonsense attitude made him both a loved and feared person to deal with. Being a science journalist, I have personally known him for the last 25 years and he was always available to speak about policy issues related to science and technology never hesitating to express sharp opinion. A hidden nugget in his long career was Menon's tight rope diplomacy that saved the tropical rain forests of Silent Valley in Kerala that were doomed to extinction due to the local State Governments insistence of making a hydroelectric dam. That single move on the directions of the then Prime Minister Indira Gandhi made Menon a darling of environmentalists. Today efforts are being made among others by Dr. M.S. Swaminathan, renowned agricultural scientist who has written to the Prime Minister Narendra Modi to rename the Silent Valley National Park as MGK Menon National Park as a tribute to the man who saved this unique ecosystem.

Alongside being a talented scientists, it is little known that he is also recognised as the person who pioneered the development of electronics in India since he was the Chairman of the Electronics Commission way back in 1971 when the electronic industry was just about taking off in a big way. From 1971-78 he served as the Secretary of the Department of Electronics. He crossed swords with some of the global multinational giants of those years like International Business Machines (IBM) to try and ensure that India be a force to reckon within the electronics industry. In fact, some even credit him for sowing the first seeds of what would be known as the information technology revolution in the coming years.

But most of his peers recognise his tenure as Director of the Tata Institute of Fundamental Research (TIFR), Mumbai for eleven long years from 1966 as the period in which TIFR the so-called cradle of Indian science was well nurtured and acquired a global recognition. Menon took over the reins of this powerhouse of Indian science at the age of 38 soon after the untimely death of the legendary Homi Jehangir Bhabha who founded TIFR.

Born on August 28, 1928 in Mangalore MGK's father was a district and sessions judge whose transferable job made him see many cities. According to a biography published in *Current Science*, "Goku's primary education took place at Kurnool and Cuddalore. Thence, the family moved to Jodhpur and he matriculated from the Punjab University in 1942. After graduating with his Bachelor of Science degree from the Agra University in 1946, while at the Jaswant College, Jodhpur, he was contemplating taking up medicine as a career. He loved science and the spark that lit his deep commitment to fundamental research was provided by none other than the Nobel Laureate C.V. Raman. As Menon himself reminisces, 'I met him [Raman] in Jodhpur when my father had invited him for a meal.... For a person in the mid-teens it was quite an experience to meet someone like him. He was exuberant and completely focused. He thumped the table and said the greatest thing for me to do in life would be to do science'. Raman had insisted that Menon should do research in physics!"

Menon then moved to the University of Bristol for his Ph.D. in elementary particle physics under the guidance of Nobel Laureate Cecil F. Powell. After returning to India in 1955, Menon joined TIFR "essentially because of Bhabha".

At TIFR Menon conducted experiments on cosmic ray particles using the specialised high altitude balloon facility. While trying to understand the physics of elementary particles, Menon was forced to go deep underground. He set up the deep underground physics laboratory in the world's deepest gold mines at Kolar in Karnataka. His efforts helped in the discovery of what are called atmospheric neutrinos. To conduct his experiments, he had to place his detectors deep inside the earth so that they can be shielded from the constant shower of cosmic rays. The thick envelope of earth above his detectors at Kolar Gold Fields helped filter out the cosmic rays.

Much to Menon's disappointment the unique experiments at Kolar Gold Fields had to be stopped since the gold mine shut down as it became un-economical and the scientists found it too expensive to keep the deep mine shafts operational. Many experts say if only the Kolar Gold Fields experiment had been continued a Nobel Prize in Physics may just have come India's way. Alas that was not to be and while speaking to me several years later Menon held no grudges against anybody.

The death of giants helped propel Menon's career, he became Director of TIFR after Dr. Bhabha's death and in 1972 Menon became Chairman of the Indian Space Research Organisation (ISRO) after the sudden passing away of Dr. Vikram Sarabhai the Father of the Indian space program.

For his contributions to the nation, Menon was conferred with prestigious national awards like Padma Shri in 1961, Padma Bhushan in 1968 and Padma Vibhushan in 1985. From 1990 to 1996 he served as a Member of Parliament and even became a Minister and was the Scientific Advisor to the Prime Minister for three years and had served as Member of the Planning Commission looking after science and technology. Menon played a key role in the setting up of the Department of Biotechnology in 1986. Menon also nurtured India's atomic energy program and served as a member of the high-powered Atomic Energy Commission.

A man who made good most of his career under the Congress regime surprised everybody when in January 1998 Menon joined the Bhartiya Janata Party but he never rose up the ranks after he switched his political affiliations. Another powerful physicist of BJP it seemed did not want another power center that could control Indian science. Menon then turned his attention to running the well-known watering hole of intellectuals in New Delhi at the India International Center where he served as President.

Ramnath Cowsik a fellow astronomer wrote Menon combined "sterling human qualities, coupled with high intellect and administrative judgement."

An asteroid '7564 Gokumenon', was named in his honour in late 2008. Today that shining scientific star of post-independent India has joined the cosmos to be remembered for ever for his contributions in making India an IT super power and a powerhouse of science and technology.

November 27, 2016

□

POLICY

35

Coming Soon a Never Before Reactor; Friendship Satellite and a New Universal Polio Vaccine: Big-Ticket Sci-Tech Push Expected in 2016

The New Year augurs well for the Indian science and technology sector. The science-friendly Prime Minister Narendra Modi is being welcomed at the annual Indian Science Congress currently being held at Mysuru, the hopes of the 10,000 strong gathering is to get an endorsement that can translate into increased budget allocations for research and development in the 2017. Science Minister Dr. Harsh Vardhan hopes his ministry will get a bigger allocation next year since he says "this year [2015-16] there was no budget cut at the time of revised estimates"' so hopes are high in Mysuru that the Finance Minister will be generous in the next fiscal.

Modi's pet theme of 'Make in India' sould reverberate through the year. The country could witness some landmark achievements in the sector, a never before Indian made new reactor could become operational; India's very own desi-global positioning system (GPS) could kick in; a reusable launch vehicle or India's first steps towards an indigenous 'Indian Space Shuttle' are likely to be lofted.

A new giant telescope could be installed at the world's highest observatory in Hanle, Ladakh. Stalled field trials of genetically modified crops could get a green signal. The year could end with a friendly neighbourhood bird in sky bringing the South Asians nations into a tighter embrace. For the *'aam admi'* an injectable polio vaccine could get wider reach in the 'end game on polio'.

The Indian space agency is preparing to undertake almost one mission every month in 2016, Herculean feat. The first quarter of the New Year could see India completing its ambitious 'desi-GPS' system. Already four of the seven satellites are in place and a basic navigation system is up and running. The months of January, February and March each could witness the last three of the seven constellation Indian Regional Navigation Satellite System (IRNSS) being launched and becoming operational soon after.

The Indian navigation system is designed to ensure better than 20-meter accuracy for navigation signals in an envelope up to 1500 kilometres from our borders, the key region where India's faces a threat perception. Only America, China, Russia have such sophisticated capabilities. This foolproof navigation system, which will always be available to India, will boost the accuracy of the jam proof Indian missiles to unprecedented levels. Average users can also expect to get desi-GPS signals on their mobile phones once suitable chips and software become widely available. The Indian system can easily be expanded to cover the entire globe if and when the country demands.

The nuclear establishment is working hard to ensure that the unit-2 of the 1000 MW nuclear reactor at Kudankulam in Tamil Nadu becomes operational. The really big event for the year could be turning on of the 500 MW Prototype Fast Breeder Reactor (PFBR) at Kalpakkam in Tamil Nadu. This would mark the coming of age of the second stage of India's ambitious atomic energy program.

The PFBR a novel Indian design has been in the making for more than a decade and runs mostly on plutonium fuel but interestingly it breeds more fuel than it consumes. A technological marvel, this reactor uses liquid sodium as a coolant, which makes the technology inherently risky. But having run a Fast Breeder Test Reactor for the last three decades the nuclear engineers are gearing up to shake the world by commissioning this mega machine in the middle of the year. Only Russia has a similar reactor operating in the world. Made at a cost of about ₹ 6000 crores some say it will produce very expensive electricity but the Department of Atomic Energy says if it succeeds, similar reactors could provide clean carbon free sustainable power to India for the next 200-300 years.

On the military side, the Indian atomic program could see the induction of India's maiden nuclear powered submarine the INS Arihant into the Indian Navy. Capable of carrying nuclear weapons, this unique underwater platform gives India the all-important second strike capability in case of a nuclear attack by an adversary.

To overcome the chronic shortage of edible oils, Indian scientists have developed a genetically modified (GM) variety of mustard. The development is stuck in the long-winded regulatory mechanism for GM products. Indian scientists are hoping that with the launch of the new 'National Biotechnology Development Strategy 2015-2020' may be a green flag could be given for the introduction of genetically modified mustard which could then become the first GM food crop to be embraced by the country.

High in the cold desert of Ladakh, India has been slowly constructing a giant telescope called Major Atmospheric Cerenkov Experiment Telescope (MACE), this specialized eye will view the universe using Gamma Rays and will be the second largest of its kind in the world but ideally placed in the world's highest observatory at Hanle perched at 4500 meters above sea level. The Electronic Corporation of India Limited is building this 24-meter diameter telescope.

The year is also likely to witness the launch of the now famous 'SAARC Satellite' the launch date for which has already been almost fixed for December 8, 2016 the anniversary of the setting up of the South Asian Association for Regional Cooperation (SAARC).

At the Sriharikota space port, on June 30, 2014 it was a moment of pride for 16,000 employees of ISRO when Modi said India has done well against odds but added *'yeh dil mange more'* (this heart wants more). He said "today, I ask our space community, to take up the challenge, of developing a SAARC Satellite—that we can dedicate to our neighbourhood, as a gift from India. A satellite, that provides a full range of applications and services, to all our neighbours. I also ask you, to enlarge the footprint of our satellite-based navigation system, to cover all of South Asia." The Indian space agency is working hard to complete the making of this communications satellite, which will cost about ₹ 235 crores and will be a gift from India to all its neighbours. Pakistan, which had initially raised some objections, is also coming around to accepting this friendly bird in the sky that will help communicate when disasters strike and help to maintain a hot line between the foreign ministries of the region.

On the health front after have vanquished wild polio from India and remaining polio free, the Ministry of Health could introduce on a countrywide basis the use of a single dose injectable polio vaccine. This the Health Minister J.P. Nadda says will give 'double protection' to our children help eliminate polio for ever, since there is still a threat of the import of the wild polio virus as two of India's neighbours Pakistan and Afghanistan still harbour this 'tiny terrorist'.

During 2015 battling odds, the Indian scientific community finally succeeded in launching an almost fully indigenous version of the so-called 'naughty boy of ISRO', the Geosynchronous Satellite Launch Vehicle (GSLV-MKII) when on August 27, 2015 the vehicle lofted India into a select club. Year 2016 could well mark India's entry into the cost-effective re-usable launch vehicle (RLV) space, as ISRO gears up for a landmark launch of the (RLV), which is really India's version of a 'Space Shuttle'.

If all goes well litany of Modi slogans 'Make in India'; 'Digital India'; 'Start-up India,' 'Stand-up India' could well get translated into tangible outcomes but for that to happen India's Finance Minister will have to open the purse strings to support the S&T sector, since growth for the Indian economy will come when research and development perks up. The scientific community is saying come on Modi, please stand up and be counted as the most science friendly Prime Minister India has ever seen. Will *'jai jawan; jai kisan* and *jai vigyan'* be the new slogan.

January 3, 2016

□

36

On Its Platinum Jubilee an Aging CSIR Cries for Renewal, but is Forced to Behave Likes a Glorified ITI!

India's largest civilian research agency the Council of Scientific and Industrial Research (CSIR) is celebrating its platinum jubilee and Prime Minister Narendra Modi is joining in the celebration on Monday, September 26, 2016. The 13,500 strong yet aging agency with 38 laboratories was looking to get a renewal instead it is being tasked with training 'school dropouts and 12th class pass students' as part of a new Integrated Skill Initiative which hopes to train some 10,000 youngsters in a year. A job for which the nearly 12,000 Industrial Training Institutes (ITI) that dot India are probably better placed to fulfil. Under the ₹ 10,000 crore skill development initiative, it is the ITIs that need to be upgraded and linked to the labs of CSIR today on the contrary top class research institutes are being diluted. India's Science Minister Dr. Harsh Vardhan defends his new proposal saying "scientists will get additional workforce through this initiative". Linking national labs to universities was probably a more viable alternative. Vardhan a staunch believer of this new push says "only 4.69 per cent of India's total workforce has undergone formal skill training, compared with 52 percent in the USA, 68 per cent in the UK, 75 per cent in Germany, 80 per cent in Japan and 96 per cent in South Korea".

CSIR has a glorious past but its future unfortunately remains hazy. The average age of a scientist in this once well-known powerhouse of industrial R&D has steadily crept up to over 50 since induction of fresh blood has literally been on a hold in the last several years. More than a decade ago it had a bench strength of about 6500 scientists today it is down to half of that and many more will be retiring soon.

A leadership crisis has been plaguing the CSIR, a year ago more than 31 of its laboratories were without full-time directors and for several years in the second term of Prime Minister Dr. Manmohan Singh even the director general's position was being filled on an *ad hoc* basis. Today with a renewed push by India's Science Minister Dr. Harsh Vardhan only three labs don't have directors. But on gender balance the agency still lags far behind with only one leadership position being held by a lady in Madhu Dikshit as Director of the Central Drug Research Institute, Lucknow.

A pioneer in its own right the mega agency is known for providing the suitable technology that gives a billion plus Indians its daily dose of salt, one scientist remarked *'aakhir jyadatar desh CSIR ka namak khata hai'*. CSIR helped track the 553 million Indians who voted in the last parliamentary elections and the tick-tock of the Indian Standard Time 1st is maintained by its laboratory. India is indeed indebted to the unknown Indian scientist who toils in the confines of it's underequipped and understaffed laboratories. On its seventy-fifth birth anniversary, the unsung stories from dingy CSIR labs that power India in the twenty first century need to be acknowledged, applauded and failures discarded.

India spends a miniscule less than one per cent of its gross domestic product on research and development but the benefits of Indian science and technology have been huge and often unrecognised. India's largest civilian research agency the Council of Scientific and Industrial Research (CSIR) is celebrating its 75th birth anniversary and it has had many successes and failures. From making India self-sufficient through reverse engineering in the early days, to making drugs that fight diseases to exploring the oceans and high Himalayas the 3500 scientists who work in 38 national laboratories make dirty coal clean and also design super computers. There have been stark failures as well like the around ₹ 400 crores the government invested in the making of India's first civilian plane Saras, both the ambitious project spearheaded by the National Aerospace Laboratories, Bengaluru and the plane itself crash landed with no gain and much pain. The much hyped Open Source Drug Discovery Program wilted just as it was gaining strength.

Earlier this year Prime Minister Narendra Modi while chairing a high level meeting on CSIR "called for laying down parameters to assess the performance of CSIR labs; and a mechanism whereby there could be internal competition among various labs. He called upon the scientific community at CSIR to list at least one hundred problems being faced by people in various parts of India, and take up the challenge of solving them technologically within a specified time period. Mentioning key areas where CSIR could take the lead in providing breakthroughs, the Prime Minister spoke of sickle cell anaemia among the tribal people, defence equipment manufacturing, life-saving equipment for the jawans, innovations related to solar energy, and innovations related to the agriculture sector." Indeed the CSIR was an early mover in solar photo voltaic technology well before the world woke up to solar energy, but a lack of support killed the initiative.

The key stone of a flourishing democracy is the single secret ballot that the Constitution empowers every adult

Indian citizen with. In 2014 Parliamentary elections, some 553 million Indian's flashed the small black-violet mark on their finger nails. Little known to many the indelible ink that we flash with flourish was first made in 1952 by the scientists of the CSIR. Every Member of Parliament who enters the hallowed portals of the Lok Sabha sports this on his nails. The secret formulation of the ink that does not fade for at least three weeks was made by the scientists of the National Physical Laboratory. It is today manufactured in a factory in Mysuru and is even helping Sri Lanka and Indonesia conduct fair democratic elections. R.A. Mashelkar, former Director General of CSIR calls the development of the indelible ink a great achievement for the preservation of India's democracy.

India was a floundering basket case with foodgrains being imported by the ship load in the early seventies from USA, then the green revolution was ushered in with the introduction of high yielding seeds, but one key catalyst was missing mechanization of farming. It was in those times of dire need that in 1974 the Central Mechanical Engineering Research Institute, Durgapur gave India its first tractor called 'Swaraj'. This robust machine has since sold more than 100,000 units and transformed India from being a net importer of foodgrains to a net exporter. It is subsequent models 'Sonalika' have also been sold in equal measure.

CSIR rose to the challenge and delivered says Girish Sahni, the Director General of CSIR recalls when "independent India had to fill its granaries to feed its hungry millions and the fledgling nation needed machines for the agricultural sector, they came from the portals of CSIR."

Affordable drug development is another rainbow in the arsenal of CSIR, fighting malaria became much easier with the development of anti-malarial drugs by the Central Drug Research Institute in Lucknow which also pioneered India's first weekly family planning pill 'Saheli'. The clot buster drug Streptokinase came from a lab in Chandigarh. The generics drug industry was pioneered by CSIR and now India has become the low cost pharmacy of the world.

The CSIR has a pan-India presence, with network of 38 national laboratories, 39 outreach centres and is home to some 3500 scientists and 3000 technical personnel with a total strength of 13,500 employees. In its hay days, it employed some 6500 scientists but in the last ten years a bar on fresh recruitments has dwindled its bench strength.

According to CSIR, "it is granted 90% of US patents granted to any Indian publicly funded R&D organization. On an average CSIR files about 200 Indian patents and 250 foreign patents per year. About 13.86% of CSIR patents are licensed—a number which is above the global average. CSIR has pursued cutting edge science and advanced knowledge frontiers. The scientific staff of CSIR only constitute about 3-4% of India's scientific manpower but they contribute to 10% of India's scientific output. In 2012, CSIR published 5007 papers in *Science Citation Index* (*SCI*) Journals with an average impact factor per paper as 2.673. In 2013, CSIR published 5086 papers in *SCI* journals with an average impact factor per paper as 2.868. CSIR is ranked at 84th among 4851 institutions worldwide and is the only Indian organization among the top 100 global institutions, according to the Scimago Institutions Ranking World Report 2014. CSIR holds the 17th rank in Asia and leads the country at the first position."

The going has not been good for CSIR it came worst off in budget increases for the current fiscal with an almost flat budget of ₹ 3600 crores. Even then there was still some reason relief since in 2015 at a meeting in Dehradun of all directors of CSIR, India's Science Minister Dr. Harsh Vardhan had pushed through a proposal that "all CSIR labs to make efforts to be self-financing in next two years". This had sent shock waves among the 16,500 staff who felt that CSIR would soon become a low cost contract research organisation pushing for private good at the cost of public good and the lofty goals of doing 'blue sky research' could be given a go by. Since then Vardhan has clarified that this was an aspirational goal and has been touring all the labs to urge scientists to conduct science that helps people.

In Modi's vision, he would like to see "CSIR oriented towards making the life of the common man better, and providing technological solutions to the problems of the poor and downtrodden sections of society". Worthy words but if scientists become social reformers who will do the cutting edge development needed for 'Made in India' not just 'Make in India'.

September 25, 2016

□

POLITICS

37

Modi *Sarkar* Anniversary: *Mangalyaan* Brought Cheers; the Monsoon could Bring Tears; while Scientists Live in Fear

Cheers, tears and fears are how one can summarize the first year in office of the Prime Minister Narendra Modi government with the promised *'Achchhe Din'* still a distant dream for the scientific community.

Mangalyaan brought cheers; the monsoon unfortunately could be playing truant twice in a row, could bring tears. However, most worrying is the fact that Indian scientists say they live in a certain fear instilled by a few summary dismissals of top boffins, like the astonishing termination of the services of the head of defence research, Avinash Chander.

Such is the despair that Raghavendra Gadagkar, President of the venerated Indian National Science Academy (INSA), New Delhi recently expressed his anguish saying 'Indian science suffers, today more than ever from government apathy.' In fact, the Modi Government's first full budget also failed to bring a smile on the faces of scientists as hikes were below expectations. Key legislations like the ones to set up a statutory regulatory mechanism for genetically modified organisms and the one to make the nuclear energy regulator independent continue to languish.

India's research and development establishment is also concerned that the high-pitched 'Make in India' campaign by Modi may actually back fire on the long standing 'Made in India' effort. Experts say unless the country owns its own intellectual property and then manufactures in India, the country could well become a cheap sweatshop for multinationals. 'Make in India' could become a sobriquet for 'Assembled in India'. In way the soft spoken Cabinet Minister for Science, Harsh Vardhan echoed that sentiment: "Make in India' needs to be translated on the ground through collaborations between the private sector which owns more than 70 per cent of the manufacturing sector and the S&T laboratories, 85 per cent of which are in the government sector."

Despite these misgivings, there is no doubt that Modi himself is a man of science, and a space buff to boot and comes across as someone who understands how innovation can be deployed for national development. Among the first six people, Modi met, as Prime Minister was C.N.R. Rao, well-known chemist and recent Bharat Ratna. Surprisingly since then Rao has been almost been sidelined and the high profile 'Scientific Advisory Council to the Prime Minister' he headed has not been reconstituted.

Modi is a huge risk taker; it was most evident when he wearing a red waistcoat he showed up before dawn on September 24, 2014 in the control room of the Indian Space Research Organisation (ISRO) in Bengaluru when the *Mangalyaan* was being steered into the Martian orbit.

His gamble paid off! India made history by becoming the first nation in the world to reach the Red Planet in its maiden attempt, and at a cost less than the making of the Hollywood blockbuster movie *Gravity*. A feat not achieved even by space giants like Russia, USA. The stacks were loaded heavily against India, and in his speech, Modi said he was advised not to go to the control room since the chances of failure were very high. In his inimitable style, he said "if it fails it is my first responsibility to be amongst you [more so since] we have achieved the near impossible" and [now] Mars has found its 'MOM'!

Incidentally not known to many as Chief Minister of Gujarat Modi visited the ISRO facilities in his home state dozens of times using the satellites to monitor the development claims of his district staff. Complacent civil servants need to be aware that the 'big brother' is now watching from the South Block as Modi is also the Minister for Space and helps steer the world's largest constellation of civilian remote sensing satellites.

Modi is truly a hands on Prime Minister within weeks of taking over he personally visited the Bhabha Atomic Research Centre in Mumbai on July 21, 2014 and along with his National Security Advisor Mr. Ajit Doval he spent a whole afternoon being briefed on India's nuclear capabilities. He took a tour of the Indian made 'Dhruva Reactor' which undoubtedly played a critical role in India becoming a nuclear weapons power. After his visit, Modi said "the success was especially creditable because it took place in the face of decades of international technology denial regime". By personally visiting India's main nuclear weapons laboratory, it can be safely inferred that Modi did even better than the iconic former BJP Prime Minister Atal Bihari Vajpayee who ordered the Pokharan nuclear tests as soon as he took power in New Delhi in 1998.

There was a growing feeling before the 2014 elections that the Bhartiya Janata Party (BJP) if it came to power it might renege on the Indo-US civilian nuclear deal as it had vehemently protested against it when it was in opposition. Nevertheless, when Modi wearing his monogrammed suit met his 'friend Barrack' in January 2015 he made classic summersault terming it the 'centrepiece' of strategic relations. Since then favourable atomic diplomacy has taken place in Canada, France and Australia.

On the space front more evidence of Indo-US bonhomie, Finance Minister Arun Jaitley for the first time earmarked ₹ 50 crore for the joint climate monitoring satellite to be made by NASA and ISRO called NISAR a high-tech synthetic aperture radar imaging satellite to be launched around 2020. Evidence of the great 'Hanuman leap' by USA, from trying to strangulate ISRO through sanctions, today America seeks to partner.

There is also evidence of somecross talk in the Modi Government, Science Minister Harsh Vardhan continues to egg the scientific community repeatedly asserting that "India will launch its first astronaut in space by 2021". A fact that ISRO denies totally since the Modi Government was yetto approve the human space flight program that would cost upwards of ₹ 12,500 crores.

Another key sector of defence research had its fair share of joys and sorrows, with the successful flights of the Agni-5 Missile, Nirbahaya Missile and the induction of the Tejas being important milestones. But the unprecedented 'termination of the contract' of the highly regarded missile scientist Avinash Chander as the head of the Defence Research and Development Organisation (DRDO) in the middle of his extended service, left a bad after taste.

The 'termination' could be correct in law, but the disrespectful manner in which the announcement was handled by Defence Minister Manohar Parikkar left much to be desired, Chander was informed of this stunning development by the media. Subsequently, a hurt Chander said "sacking is not the word one wants to hear after 41 years of service to the nation". Another summary and unprecedented rejection of the director selected for the prestigious Tata Institute of Fundamental Research (TIFR), Mumbai also sent a chill down the spine of scientists. The scientific workforce today lives in fear, demoralized at witnessing such a shabby treatment being meted out to top notch scientists.

Today, India's best-known civilian research establishment the Council of Scientific and Industrial Research (CSIR) has been without a full-time head for more than a year, its current stopgap head M.O. Garg told *Nature* magazine that the national innovation system was being affected, because of these many vacancies. In fact, the Indian Council of Medical Research (ICMR) is also bereft of a full-time leader. A certain leadership crisis has begun to set in.

However, to its credit, the Modi Government has made an effort to weed out the crony appointments system that pervaded the system operating through secretive handpicked 'selection committees'. Today more than ever posts are being advertised and a lot of that credit should flow possibly to Jitendra Singh who is Minister in the Department of Personnel and Training who for a short time was also the country's Science Minister. Singh in his brief tenure also oversaw the big hike in monthly fellowships for Indian research students, on the eve of Diwali he announced that the average monthly stipend would go up by about sixty per cent.

The biggest headache for the Modi Government in the coming months could be the mercurial moods of the monsoon, which is predicted to be 'below normal'. Last year's monsoon was a failure, resulting in a drought with a short fall of 12% in rainfall and then the double whammy of unseasonal rains earlier this year, led to an unforeseen agrarian crisis, so much so that the Modi Government is being called 'anti-farmer' by Rahul Gandhi. A back-to-back failure of the monsoon is rare but it could well spell the beginning of the end of the promised '*Achchhe Din*'. In those desperate times, it is the scientific strength that helps overcome the odds.

May 22, 2015

□

38

Modi's Gift a *Mangalyaan* in Every Hand!

The success of Prime Minister Narendra Modi's surgical strike of unearthing black money rides on the fame of the *Mangalyaan*! His government has literally decided to give a *Mangalyaan* in every person's hand by engraving a motif of the famous satellite on the new currency note. The same way as India's maiden mission to mars gladdened the hearts of Indians filling them with nationalistic pride, the move to demonetise high value notes is instilling a hope in lay people that the economy may now be lifted into a new orbit.

Sources in the Ministry of Finance have confirmed that from among several choices, Prime Minister Narendra Modi, a known space buff, hand-picked the placement of *Mangalyaan* on the new currency note. It is no secret that Modi is a great fan of the Indian Space Research Organisation (ISRO). *Mangalyaan* truly represents the 'Make in India' spirit. Though the first Indian satellite to be featured on a currency note was 'Aryabhata', India's first satellite launched in 1975 and it got pride of place on a Rupees two denomination note.

Today, India's historic maiden mission to Mars, the *Mangalyaan* has been immortalized in its life time as it finds place on the spanking new Rupees two thousand currency note. Nobody doubts that it is one of India's greatest achievements in technology in recent times. The mission continues to remain active and still beams back data three years after it was launched.

On that historic morning on September 24, 2014 when *Mangalyaan* entered the orbit of the Red Planet, Modi made it a point to be present in the control room of ISRO to boost the morale of the scientists and has since exclaimed that the making of the mission at ₹ 450 crores or about $67 million the spacecraft was cheaper than the making of the Hollywood blockbuster movie *Gravity*.

The currency note carries a motif of what ISRO officially calls the Mars Orbiter Mission (MOM) but interestingly the government in its wisdom has inscribed the word '*Mangalyaan*' on the currency note. Here lies a hidden tale on the naming of the spacecraft.

The first official announcement that India was heading to Mars came in 2012 when Prime Minister Manmohan Singh in his Independence Day speech delivered in Hindi from the ramparts of the 17th century Red Fort in New Delhi gave a clarion call while also christening it, and said "*Mangalyaan* will be a big step in science technology".

Interestingly, the official English translation of the speech released by the government did not have the word '*Mangalyaan*' anywhere in it and in its wisdom ISRO continued to argue that the spacecraft was never christened '*Mangalyaan*' but anyone who heard that speech or still cares to listen to the recorded speech available on You Tube can again confirm it.

Prime Minister Manmohan Singh's speeches that were delivered in Hindi were actually written for delivery in Urdu recall he was born in a part of Punjab now in Pakistan and had his early education where Urdu was the dominant language. If one carefully sees the turning of the pages on the lectern at the Red Fort they go in the 'opposite direction' since Urdu is read from the right to left.

Not just ISRO many in the media made a joke that a specialist like myself was repeatedly referring the mission by the 'nickname *Mangalyaan*' and not its official name MOM. This was a needless controversy then and it has been finally laid to rest by the Indian Government officially making the name '*Mangalyaan*' unforgettable on the new currency note.

Since his days as Chief Minister of Gujarat Modi has had a fascination about space technology. In his speech from the control room of ISRO, Modi had passionately exclaimed "today mars has found its mom" adding "history has been created today. We have dared to reach out into the unknown. And have achieved the near impossible." So his choice of placing an artistic representation of *Mangalyaan* did not come as a surprise to some who know of his deep involvement in using the fruits of modern science to help the common man.

Designing a secure currency note is an art, speaking about it Shaktikanta Das a Secretary in the Ministry of Finance said it took them 3-4 months to make the new currency note and today only 2-3 specialists have the requisite expertise.

In the first few hours, there was another controversy related to ISRO on the new ₹ 2000 note, some reports erroneously suggested that the government had embedded a 'nano GPS chip for easy tracking of the notes' and that India's regional satellite navigation system Navic would do the needful. Kiran Kumar, Chairman ISRO had immediately called the bluff telling this correspondent "this was a figment of someone's fertile imagination". Later it was confirmed by the government that there is no embedded chip on the currency note.

Today from its active perch some 225 million kilometres away from Earth the *Mangalyaan* must be smiling looking at the fuss being created in India as 1.30 billion people scramble to lay their hands on the *Mangalyaan*. It may be reminded in that same speech Modi had also said "grasp the idea of *Shunya* or nothingness" which is what the demonetisation is likely to do to those running the economy in the black market.

November 13, 2016

□

39

Back to the Future from Food Rationing to Cash Rationing!

Making and breaking queues is a human game Indians love to play. Ubiquitous ration queues thanks to 'Ship to Mouth' became a passé long ago but today queues due to 'ATM to Mouth' is the new game India is learning to play.

In his inimitable style, Prime Minister Narendra Modi has repeatedly emphasized of 'start-up India and stand up India' today both are happening in good measure people are starting up early morning in search of for currency notes and they are also standing up in long queues may be Modi should add a new phrase 'Queue up India'. This is not the India the people of this country dreamt off.

India is undoubtedly a country of long queues and why not with a population of 1.3 billion serpentine lines is a normal sight. Today it seems at least one person from every household is standing patiently looking for that piece of paper which says 'I promise to the pay the bearer the sum of one hundred Rupees'.

The world's largest democracy has literally become cashless ever since that fateful Tuesday announcement by Modi to suck eighty-six per cent of the currency from the hands that toil for India. Currency is the life blood of any nation and if you suck eighty-six per cent of the life of person sooner than later the person is likely to pass out.

Just the other day a neighbour was buying vegetable using a handful of loose coins that had dollars thrown in for good measure. '*Ek Naya paisa*' got an all new meaning after that fateful 8 pm announcement.

As Finance Minister Arun Jaitley emphasizes repeatedly 'India is the fastest growing large economy of the world', but what is growing thick and fast are the long queues and people's patience is running out in this new unprecedented '*Shirshasana*' or a headstand the common man has been made to do by the Yoga-loving Modi.

Indians know how to handle the rough and tumble of daily life and many are supportive of the move of Modi to rein in the shadow economy that ran on cash transactions. India is indeed a country of contrasts we can send the Tata Nano Car sized *Mangalyaan* hurtling 200 million kilometres away to hit bull's eye in orbiting the Red Planet but we can't ensure that average Indians get their hard earned ₹ 2000 without having to jostle.

The serpentine queues are lining up to take modern India back to the future it seems! To me a small town country boy this brings back memories of when India was living 'Ship to Mouth'...queues at ration shops extended till infinity and stocks vanished faster than they were ever replenished.

Today, I go back four decades ago to a time when food shortages were plenty, grains like wheat were being imported in millions of tons from the United States of America under the 'PL 480' or food for peace scheme and since they landed on seaside ports the phrase 'Ship to Mouth' became a household name.

I recall my mother tightly holding my little finger and both of us queueing up outside a dilapidated ration shop to buy a few kilograms or red-coloured wheat and a handful of sugar. More often than not a handwritten placard read 'out of stock' very akin to the scribbles on paper that today reads 'no cash'.

Ration shops and queues were a part of the daily lexicon in the bad old days of the twentieth century when the left of center socialistic Congress Party led-governments had brute majority. Today after decades another majority government albeit right of centre rules and is considered rather friendly to capitalism and trade, yet queues are back in vogue. But even in this so-called resurgent digital India of the twenty first-century where 'Make in India' is prevailing slogan the country is literally 'making queues' and this time it seems it is for 'ATM to Mouth'! Patience is running thin and a hungry India may soon become an angry India.

Food rationing was rampant, households usually converged at 'ration shops' and not at Automatic Teller Machines (ATMs). Back then money may not have been plenty but at least it was there but foodgrains were in short supply. Today the new generation has learnt to be patient in queues in 'Food Courts' but now loose change is in severe short supply and credit card machines are jammed as the servers are unable to handle the new digital rush.

Banks have become the new ration shops, and the talk of the neighbourhood revolves around the fact that is such and such person hit a jackpot he was able to withdraw a princely sum of ₹ 2000 from the always parched ATM machines. It is almost like the long-forgotten lottery has made a comeback.

Doomed we may not be but troubled we certainly are since on the issue of demonetisation the government started off by asking for two days, Jaitley then said bear with me the trauma will continue for two weeks and now a tearful Modi extended the pain to two months.

Eyes wide open India has blindly opted a bumpy route to a cashless economy all in the hope that the elusive black money holder will be ensnared. Indeed it seems we are country that is heading back to the future as we race to become a cashless economy waiting patiently in never ending queues collecting as doles rationed cash which is rightfully our own. The government it seems is blind to the fact that black money holders don't stand in queues to liquidate their ill-gotten wealth.

A so-called surgical strike on black money by the Modi Government whose script is now unfortunately going horribly wrong in its implementation. On the ground it is causing too just much disruption for the vast majority of honest Indians. Cash rationing was not a gift that people expected when Modi promised *'achhe din'*.

November 20, 2016

□

40

Israeli Prime Minister, Benjamin Netanyahu's 'entrepreneurial' advice to PM Narendra Modi on 'Start-up India, Stand-up India'

If Prime Minister Narendra Modi's Independence Day dream of India succeeding as 'Start Up' country has to get kick-started, there is a lot to learn from the original 'Start Up Nation' Israel. The tiny country of Israel mushrooms almost two new start-up companies everyday and today houses some 5000 start-ups. New Delhi, of course, is just starting up!

On being asked by this columnist if Modi's call for a 'start up India' can succeed, Benjamin Netanyahu, Prime Minister of Israel, recently said, 'as far as the 'start up nation' I think this has a lot to do with entrepreneurial spirit. I have noticed that in Silicon Valley [USA], you hear Indian dialects and you hear Hebrew, sometimes you hear some English, which means there is a lot [happening]. There is a lot of spirit for enterprise in both our countries.' Speaking in Jerusalem, he also added that he expects 'a lot' from Indo-Israeli relations and that he was 'anxious to meet Prime Minister Modi again in September in the UN just a few weeks away.' Meanwhile, in a few weeks, President Pranab Mukherjee is expected to visit Israel and when that happens, he would make history by becoming the first Indian head of state to ever visit Israel. Israeli diplomats in

Jerusalem say Mukherjee will definitely be given a flavour of the huge innovation capacity of Israel.

The desert blooms start-ups.

Mushrooms find it hard to grow in the arid environment of Israel, but start-ups mushroom all over, in garages, in attics in glib office buildings in basements of university cafeteria; in this holy land, it is hard to cast a stone that may not hit a start up somewhere.

One such top-notch firm is located in the heart of the Negev Desert where due to the dry heat, nothing really grows, yet enterprise flourishes irrigated by the human brain. Jerusalem Venture Partners (JVP) is rated one of the best in the world in its domain. It nurtures and grows infant ideas and in the last four years, it helped create 120 companies worth 1.3 billion dollars. Today, its affiliate JVP Cyber Labs is working on the hot topic of cyber security, which Israel believes is an untapped market.

In Israel, they don't talk about how their cyber sleuths allegedly used the 'Stuxnet', a computer virus to attack and disable the uranium enrichment plants of Iran, but what the Jewish experts do talk about is how vulnerable are the smart phones we use almost like lifelines. They emphasise how identity theft should worry almost anybody who uses the Internet. Israeli cyber experts suggest that open Wifi connections are some of the most vulnerable and easy conduits for cyber thefts.

This start-up JVP Cyber Labs is working on how to make mobile data communication safer. The concept of mobile wallets is yet to catch up in India, but with the rampant seeding of Aadhar numbers and once they get linked to bank accounts and the direct transfer of benefits becomes common place, at that point, cyber security of smart phones and anti-hacking software will have to be put in place by all and sundry. A fertile market for the 900 million mobile phones that dot India.

Meanwhile, what gives Israel a unique start-up ecosystem? It is not the economy, stupid it is the culture! Mr. Yoav Tzruya, Partner, JVP Cyber Labs, Beer Sheva, Israel says 'one of the basic cultural differences that exist in Israel as a start-up nation is how we look at failure. In Israel, we do not penalise failure per se; we look at the entrepreneurs who have created their companies that have failed as people who have gained from their experience. We have been asked by many countries around the world to replicate it, the successful model of innovation and always culture was an obstacle, people that founded start-up and failed were looked down upon. It is critical actually to embrace failure, learn from it rather than look down upon it.' Enthused by Modi's latest call, JVP is planning to open an India operation.

To encourage more global companies to learn about the exciting start-up environment, the Israeli government organises a road show what it calls 'Start Tel Aviv'. This global event brings together start-ups from different countries to take part in an intense, five-day start-up experience. Next to be held in September where one Indian company 'Audio Compass', an Indian start-up that makes software which transforms regular smart phones into a personal audio tour guide helping tourists get a flavour of what they see, it will showcase its product in Israel.

Ms. Ditza Froim, Minister Counsellor, an Israeli diplomat at the Embassy of Israel, said, "Ideas, dreams and willingness to take chances are the pillars of innovation and entrepreneurship. For Israel, these are the essence of our existence and the pillars of our security, society, culture and economy. Israel has established a vibrant sustainable economy with GDP per capita of about USD 37,000, a global leader in the field of agriculture and a hot-house for innovations, entrepreneurship and start-ups. Through its human capital, Israel generates more start-up companies than large, industrial nations, like Japan, China, Korea, Canada, Germany and the UK. In addition, Israel has attracted per capita, over twice as much venture capital investment as the US and 30 times more than all the members of the European Union combined.'

Modi may want to learn a little publicised secret of how Israel nurtures the start-up environment. It does it through incubators that are set up by the Israeli government. These special purpose vehicles give $ 600,000 risk-free loan to the promising start-ups. It may come as a big surprise but if companies fail, they do not need to pay back the loan but if they succeed, they pay back a 3% annual royalty.

In India, on the other hand, if the Modi government were to extend such a facility, the Comptroller and Auditor General of India (CAG) would ask so many questions that sooner than later, on prime time television, the 'nation would want an answer' as to how such a big scam took place under the command of the prime minister.

Another big reason for Israel's success as a start-up nation is the tight embrace between companies, university researchers and entrepreneurs. If Prime Minister Modi's mission of 'start-up India' has to succeed the country as a whole will have to change the way Indians view failures. Even in Israel, not all start-ups make it big, but then disappointments are viewed positively truly in the spirit of failures being the stepping stones to success and this probably what makes Israel a powerhouse of innovation. On your upcoming visit to Israel, Modi, please conduct a town hall meeting between Indian and Israeli entrepreneurs to gain from each other in a win-win partnership.

August 30, 2015

□

SPACE

41

America Looks to Partner in India's Quest for Deep Space Exploration! As India goes Planet Hunting, ISRO Eyeing Venus, Mars and Asteroid

An Indo-US deep space exploration mission is in the offing! The unthinkable is already happening in space, India and America are together planning to explore the last unknown frontier. Until recently India was an untouchable.

Venus, Mars, and an Asteroid all could be the next big destinations that India will be exploring. The Indian Space Research Organisation (ISRO) is now embarking on a new planet-hunting endeavour. There are indications that the United States of America will be working with India in this 'deep space exploration'.

As per ISRO's own plans, in the next few years another robust mission to planet Mars is being planned by ISRO. A possible flyby to an asteroid is likely. A small satellite aptly called 'Aditya' will keep a constant eye on the ever-changing moods of the Sun.

Speaking to students of Indian Institute of Technology, Chennai Richard Verma, Ambassador of USA to India sprung a surprise by saying "we look forward to path-breaking work between NASA [National Aeronautics and

Space Administration] and ISRO on deep space exploration to Mars and beyond".

Till 2005, ISRO was a total pariah kept under full technology denial and sanctions were in full force but a decade later the chill has gone and relations have thawed, now hand-in-hand both want to fly 'where no man has gone before'.

If Pluto was the target for the American space agency through its mission 'New Horizons', the Indian space agency is also setting its goals to explore the Solar System to its limits. On ISRO's wish list 'a technology demonstration mission or a flyby to the outer solar system'.

The current ISRO chief who played a key role in the success of *Mangalyaan* says "for the next planetary mission, we are looking at opportunities whether it is a repeat Mars mission, or Venus mission or even an Asteroid mission" revealed Kiran Kumar, Chairman, Indian Space Research Organisation (ISRO).

Exploring Venus could be the next logical step as India has already been to Mars. It is Earth's neighbour and if all goes well in a few years an Indian rocket will lift off and head towards the inside of the Solar System. Until date only Russia, America, the European Space Agency (ESA) are the ones to have successfully reached Venus, in 2010 Japan tried but failed. Can India make global history once again by becoming the first Asian country to reach Venus. Repeating a moment in history when India's *Mangalyaan* in its maiden attempt itself reached the Red Planet a feat not achieved by any other country.

Venus is considered a twin of Earth and yet very little is understood about this terrestrial planet. It is almost the same size that of Earth but it has a hugely dense atmosphere made up mostly of carbon dioxide and being closer to the Sun it has an average temperature of about 460°C. U.R. Rao, former Chairperson of ISRO and head of the committee that decides on scientific missions has long expressed a desire that India should ideally soon head to Venus.

It is believed by experts that Venus in a way resembles what could be the ultimate fate of Earth if runaway release of carbon dioxide goes on unabated and the climate continues to change with carbon dioxide being amassed in the atmosphere. Kumar says there are many things to be learned at Venus like trying to figure out "why does the atmosphere of Venus rotate in the opposite direction".

Some of these future planetary mission would need bigger rockets and towards that Kumar says India's indigenously made Geosynchronous Satellite Launch Vehicle Mark-II (GSLV Mk-II) is probably going to be the preferred vehicle as it has 'superior capabilities'. The almost 50 meter tall rocket that weighs as much as 414 ton is capable of hoisting a 2500-kilogram satellite on inter-planetary voyages.

India has had hugely successful interplanetary missions, the most recent being *Mangalyaan* that reached the Martian orbit in 2014 and continues to operate with vigour sending back scientific data to India. The Mars Orbiter Mission or MOM was launched using the Polar Satellite Launch Vehicle (PSLV). Kumar says "we have demonstrated the overall capability that we can go up to Mars with a minimal launcher using the PSLV".

Therefore, a repeat mission to Mars is very likely but with a heavier satellite where scientific instruments would get priority. Kumar says "the next mission will be science driven."

A recent document submitted by ISRO to the government enlists what is going through the minds of the scientists and engineers at ISRO: "Initiatives towards undertaking a Mars orbiter and lander mission during 2018-launch opportunity-identification of scientific payloads. Exploration of Mars surface features' viz. morphology, topography, mineralogy and Martian atmosphere" all can be studied in *Mangalyaan-2*. Kumar says no final decision has been taken on the next Mars mission and no date has been fixed. Kumar is sure that *Mangalyaan-2* will be a science mission unlike the first *Mangalyaan*, which was a 'technology demonstrator'.

India already has a second visit to the Moon planned for 2018 through *Chandrayaan-2* that will include an orbiter, lander and a rover on the lunar surface. This ₹ 500 crore mission is already being put together in Bengaluru and it will be launched using the GSLV Mk-II. According to ISRO, it would "further our understanding of origin and evolution of the Moon with improved versions of *Chandrayaan-1* instruments for imaging, mineralogy and chemistry; addition of alpha and neutron spectrometers in the orbiter. Studies of lunar radiation environment including solar wind interactions." Beyond *Chandrayaan-2* ISRO seeks to plan for "lunar sample return missions from the polar region of moon and a possible establishment of lunar observatory".

ISRO in its plans also lists 'a remote sensing asteroid orbiter and comet flyby: with the science goal of understanding the evolution of asteroids and comets, early solar system processes, meteorite-asteroid connection, physical and chemical properties of asteroid and cometary material.'

India is also seeking to undertake a visit to an asteroid and there is every possibility that India may cooperate with the American space agency, NASA on its asteroid initiative where it will try to re-direct or even harvest an asteroid. India with its demonstrated capabilities of undertaking low cost high value interplanetary travel—*Mangalyaan* at ₹ 450 crores was the cheapest mission ever—offers great opportunities for NASA to work with. A possible win-win for both sides where space science would be the biggest gainer.

July 19, 2015

□

42

India and China Set Their Eyes on a Joint Satellite Constellation even as Pakistan Bails Out of SAARC Satellite

Space really knows no national boundaries, yet some of the most-bitter earthly battles are fought on space issues. Amidst this so-called star wars, some new green shoots of international collaboration can be seen to be emerging.

Most recently, possibly the short-sightedness of Pakistan led it to opt out of the proposed SAARC Satellite, a friendly gift from India. From its ashes, it seems a new proposal to have satellite constellation on behalf of the BRICS nations (Brazil, Russia, India, China and South Africa) has emerged.

Meanwhile, the 11 of the world's best-known and richest space agencies met this week in New Delhi and have mooted the idea of a 'global space observatory' to monitor climate change. It seems some of the existential questions on the future of humankind can best be answered from the inky darkness of space. Jean-Yves LeGall, the head of the French space agency (CNES) says "the need of the hour is for the space agencies to pool their resources" to create a "virtual constellation of earth observing satellites" that will monitor global warming and climate change.

A BRICS Constellation Emerges

India lost its western neighbour Pakistan from the proposed 'SAARC Satellite' but has now managed to gain China the eastern giant in the proposed 'BRICS Constellation of satellites'. The cat was let out of the bag by Mr. YanHua Wu, Deputy Administrator for the Chinese National Space Agency (CNSA) who was in India this week to participate in a space summit hosted in New Delhi. Wu said "we have been in dialogue with India on the BRICS Constellation for disaster risk reduction". Details of the proposed BRICS satellite constellation are still sketchy but Dr. Kiran Kumar, Chairman of the Indian Space Research Organisation (ISRO) hinted that "a virtual remote sensing satellite constellation for the BRICS nations" was on the anvil.

It is interesting that the two regional space powers India and China who are as some observers believe locked in a 21st century Asian Space Race, are now hoping to join hands to combat the threat of climate change. Both India and China have cooperated extensively in trying to negotiate an amenable Paris Agreement on Climate Change. Now it seems the threat of a warming globe is getting the two space powers to warm up to each other.

China and India both have end-to-end capabilities in space, yet China has a huge edge as it launched its first astronaut way back in 2003 and has heavier lift rockets in its arsenal. India was beaten to the moon orbit by China when it sent its Chang'e-1 satellite to the moon in 2007. India did out pace China in reaching the orbit of Mars in 2014 with *Mangalyaan*. Nevertheless, now the threat of climate change is making the two Asian giants, which among them house 2.5 billion people to come together and collaborate.

It seems the first step for a BRICS Constellation was initiated at a meeting held in the Austrian capital Vienna earlier this year. According to the CNSA, its deputy administrator participated in the meeting, which was held under the auspices of the United Nations Office for Outer Space Affairs and was attended by more than two dozen participants. Sources from CNSA report that "at the meeting, the BRICS countries confirm their willingness to participate in the construction of the virtual constellation". The motivation from CNSA it seems is that "the successful implementation of remote sensing satellite constellation BRICS countries, will further enrich the content of cooperation BRICS countries to strengthen national cohesion". Most importantly, the CNSA believes the BRICS Constellation would "enhance China's international voice and influence in the field of aerospace."

It is interesting that India space scientists who understand the deep capabilities of the Chinese have not rebuffed this proposal, since both neighbours have a lot to learn from each other. Both Indian and Chinese space programs are largely indigenously developed as home grown efforts as both the neighbours have independently suffered under long drawn out technology denial and sanctions regimes especially from the United States of America.

After having unsuccessfully scuttled the space programs of both India and China for long, now America is trying to embrace the same international partners, hoping that the emerging giants would dole out resources as NASA's own budget stagnates and ambitions soar to putting 'boots on Mars by 2030'.

Speaking in New Delhi at the space summit General Charles Bolden the Head of the National Aeronautics and Space Administration (NASA), Washington DC said "our planet is a fragile oasis in the blackness of space...the partnerships are getting stronger and I have no doubt that the coming decades will find us with new capabilities to explore, human beings at new and farther destinations, a greater understanding of our home planet and greater unity among humanity."

SAARC Satellite Dies a Premature Death

India's far-reaching proposal of gifting a friendly bird in the sky to the eight countries of the South Asian Association for Regional Cooperation (SAARC) died a premature death as Pakistan dropped out of the proposal saying it already has 'advanced capabilities in space'. That Pakistan rebuffed India's gift was confirmed by the Ministry of External Affairs when it issued a statement saying "Pakistan has decided to opt out of the SAARC Satellite which will now be called the South Asian Satellite".

On a visit to ISRO, Prime Minister Narendra Modi had mandated ISRO to fly a satellite that would aid better communication especially during natural disasters. This 'South Asian Satellite' would weigh nearly 2000 kg having 12 Ku band transponders with a footprint spanning across South Asia. It seems all the seven nations in South Asia, Bangladesh, Bhutan, India, Maldives, Nepal, Afghanistan and Sri Lanka have agreed to work together to enjoy the benefits of the 'South Asian Satellite' which is essentially a communications satellite with as of now no remote sensing capabilities. That Pakistan's space agency the Space and Upper Atmosphere Research Commission (SUPARCO) advised Islamabad to 'opt out' was surprising since this would have been the first time it would have gotten a toe hold with anything to with the Indian space agency. The South Asian Satellite is being fabricated at ISRO's satellite centre in Bengaluru and will be launched later this year on an incredible journey that would bond the neighbours in space forever.

As Bolden told a crowd of 750 space scientists in New Delhi "we are on an incredible journey together today—a journey of breath taking exploration and that is probably the greatest thing that exploration does – it brings us together… [this is about] about turning science fiction into science fact and making the impossible possible."

Modi no doubt did try to make the impossible possible by extending on a friendly no-cost basis India's advanced capabilities in space to its smaller rival and neighbour Pakistan. Despite, Islamabad having waged wars on New Delhi and its continued tacit support in aiding and abetting cross border terrorism on India. On the otherhand, science fiction could well turn into science fact, if rivals India and China do forge a partnership in sharing space technology.

April 10, 2016

□

43

ISRO's Big Leap Embarks on Launching an Indian Space Shuttle!

For the very time in its history the Indian Space Research Organisation (ISRO) is actually growing wings as it embarks this month on a never before space flight that would make history. The Indian space agency is all set to undertake the maiden launch of its very own indigenously version of a 'Space Shuttle', a fully made in India effort. Today a sleek-winged body almost the weight and size of a sports utility vehicle (SUV) is being given final touches at Sriharikota awaiting the final countdown.

Yes, the big powers abandoned the idea of a winged reusable launch vehicle but India's frugal engineers believe the solution to reducing cost of launching satellites into orbit is to recycle the rocket or make it re-usable. Scientists at ISRO believe that they could reduce the cost of launching stuff into space by as much as ten times if reusable technology succeeds bringing it down to $2000 per kilogram.

Very soon and if all goes well possibly before the monsoon sets in, India's space port at Sriharikota on the coast of the Bay of Bengal in Andhra Pradesh will witness the launch of the indigenously made Reusable Launch Vehicle – Technology Demonstrator (RLV-TD). This will be the first time ISRO will launch a spacecraft, which actually has delta wings and after launch it will be glided back onto a virtual runway in the Bay of Bengal.

The RLV-TD is unlikely to be recovered from sea during this experiment as it is expected that the vehicle will disintegrate on impact with water since it is not designed to float. The purpose of the experiment is not to see it float but to glide and navigate from a velocity five times higher than the speed of sound onto a designated virtual runway in the Bay of Bengal some 500 kilometres from the coast.

Very similar in its looks to the American Space Shuttle, the RLV-TD being experimented is a scale model which is almost six times smaller than the final version. Dr. K. Sivan, Director of the Vikram Sarabhai Space Center, Thiruvananthapuram says "these are just the first baby steps towards the big *Hanuman* leap". The final version will take at least 10-15 years to get ready since designing a human rated re-usable rocket is no kid stuff.

The only countries that have attempted operational flights of a space shuttle are America, which flew its Space Shuttle 135 times and then retired it in 2011 and since then it lost its capacity to send astronauts in space on American made rockets. The Russians made only a single space shuttle and called it Buran it flew into space just once in 1989. After that the French and Japanese have made some experimental flights, from available literature it seems the Chinese have never attempted a space shuttle.

India embarked on making its own version of the space shuttle by thinking about it more than 15 years ago, but work in earnest it seems started only five years ago when a dedicated team of engineers and scientists plunged into making RLV-TD a reality. The 6.5 meter long 'aeroplane'-like spacecraft will weigh 1.75 tons and will be hoisted into the atmosphere on a special rocket booster. The special booster or the first stage is powered using a solid fuel and it will hoist the RLV-TD experiment to about 70 kilometres into the atmosphere from where the descent will begin. During the descent, phase which is essentially a glider like event small thrusters will help the vehicle to be navigated onto the exact spot where it is supposed to land. Ships, satellites and radars will monitor its descent. The current experimental version has no undercarriage so it cannot be brought back onto land and India lacks a runway that is longer than five kilometres in length to accommodate such a landing.

Some private billionaires with very active support from NASA the American space agency have been trying to master vertical lift-off and vertical landing as part of trying to recycle rocket engines. Space X a company owned by Elon Musk born in South Africa is a billionaire who became big through the Internet economy has been able to land its Falcon-9 rocket onto a sea-based platform. On the same lines the company Blue Origin owned by Jeff Bezos landed its New Shepard rocket on land in Texas, USA. Bezos a billionaire made it big by building the Amazon online trading platform. In fact, recently General Charles Bolden the Chief of NASA when he was in New Delhi said today the competition has shifted to a fight among billionaires to reduce the cost of launching satellites into space.

The making of the Indian Space Shuttle or RLV-TD has taken five years and the government has invested ₹ 95 crores in the project. This flight will test the capability of the vehicle to survive a re-entry at speeds higher than that of sound so it is called a hypersonic experiment (HEX). Later in the next few flights the RLV will be subjected to a landing experiment and another return flight experiment. Once these are successful, ISRO will then decide on what should be the final configuration of the Reusable Launch Vehicle.

One key technology the scientists at VSSC had to develop was to make materials that can withstand the very high temperatures that the exterior of the vehicle is faced with as it comes back into the dense atmosphere after its journey through near vacuum in space. The friction from the air turns the exterior like a red-hot iron plate. To be able to withstand these 5000-7000°C temperature the scientists have developed very lightweight heat resistant silica tiles that are plastered on the underbelly of the so-called Indian space plane. The nose cone takes the brunt of the high temperatures and is made up of a special carbon-carbon composite that can withstand high temperature. These special materials are necessary to protect the insides of the vehicle where the temperature should never go higher than 50°C.

In fact, it is these heat-resistant tiles and thermal coating that failed on the American Space Shuttle, Columbia that resulted in the death of Indian-born American astronaut Kalpana Chawla in 2003.Consequently, ISRO has laid a lot of emphasis on the thermal management of the RLV.

After the successful deployment of the Swadeshi Global Positioning System through NAVIC or Navigation with Indian Constellation, ISRO is again reaching for the stars.

Technology development is tough and space fairing is certainly not for the faint hearted and the 600 scientists and engineers who have toiled hard in making the RLV-TD a reality will be watching with baited breath if their baby succeeds. Shyam Mohan the project director from VSSC for this landmark experiment says his team has spent sleepless nights in perfecting this new rocket but adds that space technologies are inherently risky. So will ISRO succeed where other super powers have failed, Indians certainly hope for the best, as success has become a habit at ISRO.

May be sooner than later the RLV should be named the *'Kalamyaan'* after India's legendary former President A.P.J Abdul Kalam an aeronautics engineer *par excellence* who made top class rockets and dreamt big of India being propelled to become a developed country. For ISRO no dream is too big as it carefully forges ahead to have a fully 'swadeshi space shuttle'.

May 15, 2016

□

44

ISRO's Century Emboldens it to Embrace Private Sector. But is the Love Affair One Sided?

Almost unsung the Indian Space Research Organisation (ISRO) completed a century of launching satellites in space! This was in true test cricket fashion a slow plod taking almost 36 years, since the first satellite to be launched from India was Rohini in 1980.

The Indian space agency remains not out and is now showing an inclination to play game akin to the Indian Premier League (IPL) by hitting sixers and fours in coming rocket launches.

In a bold first move' ISRO is also opening its doors to the private sector to make not just components but full satellites. This is quite a leap in space by ISRO which has till now endeavoured to fabricate all satellites in-house.

In another parallel but very significant development Team Indus a Bengaluru-based private space start-up which is attempting India's first private moon shot got a big boost when on June 29, 2016 the French Space Agency (CNES) inked an 'letter of intent' with this young bundle of energy whose motto is 'aspire, believe and create'. For the French space giant to even think of flying a high end camera on the module Team Indus seeks to send to the moon is a hugely positive movement.

Team Indus is India's only entry for the $20 million Google Lunar X Prize. Speaking the Toulouse Space Fair, Jean-Yves Le Gall President of the French space agency said "CNES must look for excellence where it is to be found, for today's space technology will drive tomorrow's technology revolutions and growth. In joining forces with Team Indus on this mission to land a rover on the Moon in 18 months' time, CNES is showing that innovation in France has a key role to play in New Space. These new players are doing things differently and working to short schedules by deploying innovative methods. The average age of our new partners is 30, so we will learn as much from them as they will from us."

Back to ISRO's big commercial success, to be precise on May 22, 2016, ISRO has launched 113 satellites into space, on this thirty-sixth mission of the Polar Satellite Launch Vehicle (PSLV) it sent in one go 20 birds soaring into space in a perfect mission. There was no overt celebration of the achievement of the century and the understated Chairman of ISRO Dr. A.S. Kiran Kumar simply said 'a job done'.

This was also a hugely significant launch since for the first time ISRO launched 17 foreign satellites all on commercial basis. Interestingly, 13 of these small satellites were from United States of America which shows the growing confidence the American entities have on the Indian launcher.

Most importantly for reasons of commerce when a whiff of privatisation seems to be drifting through ISRO, there was one satellite that was from the stable of the Internet giant Google. The 110 kg earth imaging Sky Sat Gen 2-1 satellite is owned by Terra Bella a Californian company owned by Google. This was the first time an Indian 'new space' start-up called Earth2Orbit (E2O) negotiated the launch contract on behalf of Google and Antrix Corporation. Suggesting Indian private companies are beginning to show a mark.

Susmita Mohanty the Chief Executive Officer of E2O, Bengaluru said "this is a Berlin-wall moment in [Indian] space history which will pave the way for more American launches on the PSLV and enable other Indo-US commercial space engagements in the future". Who adds the launch represents a landmark in space-related collaboration between the world's two largest democracies. Terra Bella is the first commercial American satellite operator to secure a launch contract with the Indian Government. Earth2Orbit (E2O) was instrumental in pioneering this historic first. Further adding that the launch was a resounding success. It represents the initial catalyst moment in which both countries increasingly collaborate in both civil and commercial space advances. The proverbial floodgates of this, new to India, commercial US satellite market are now open and one can see possibilities of exciting new waves of collaborative activity in this sector.

While ISRO is heavily focussed on meeting the national requirements, but as when there is access capacity it is made available on a commercial basis. As a consequence till early this year ISRO had earned nearly $100 million by launching some 57 satellites for 20 countries. This is only the beginning since the launch market is estimated to be a multi-billion dollar market.

Since the turn of the century when Dr. K. Kasturirangan was the Chairman of ISRO, the Indian space agency has been making noises that it seeks to hive of the PSLV to the private sector, but not much movement has taken place even a few months ago ISRO made a renewed call that it seeks to focus on making new technology and that repeat launches should be taken over the industry. ISRO feels the industry can utilize the launch port of Sriharikota but the private industry should make the PSLV. Towards this the engineering giant Larsen & Toubro or L&T had evinced interest but not much movement seems to have taken place.

Even today the bulk of the components for the rocket are actually supplied by the private sector but the final assembly is still done by specialists from ISRO. In a renewed push the Kumar has made a clarion call that the first private sector launch could take place as early as 2020 from Sriharikota. But it still remains to be seen which Indian industry or an industry consortium bites the bait.

On the satellite front a day after the hugely successful launch ISRO organised a meeting at the ISRO satellite centre in Bengaluru where 110 aerospace industries participated where ISRO made the surprise announcement that the private industry should make full satellite.

This bold move came as part of the "Conference on Enabling Spacecraft Systems Realisation through Industries" orgaized in Bengaluru on June 23, 2016. According to ISRO, the conference was organised to elicit industry support for spacecraft realisation on an end-to-end basis to meet the rapidly increasing national demand for space-based services and the realisation of Prime Minister Narendra Modi's objective of 'Make in India'.

In a statement ISRO said "over the years, a number of Indian Industries have been actively participating in realising various subsystems of spacecraft. A variety of models have been adopted by ISRO in outsourcing jobs to these vendors. However, end-to-end realisation of spacecraft has not yet been realised. The conference aimed to fill this gap."

Kumar told the delegates that almost all the government departments and ministries had evinced keen interest in applying space technology for carrying out their mandates. In order to meet the increased demand for space-based services, it was imperative that ISRO joined hands with the industries in its effort towards enhancing its capacity. He also impressed upon the delegates about India's great potential to capture a sizeable portion of the business in the international space market.

Participating in the industry meeting Dr. M. Annadurai, Director, of the ISRO Satellite Centre spoke "about the need for launching at least 10-12 satellites every year." He stressed that this goal would necessarily have to be driven by a synergetic collaboration between ISRO and industry since such a partnership would be a win-win situation for both. Dr. Annadurai also announced that "the Expression of Interest (EoI) for realising spacecraft on an end-to-end basis has been hosted on ISRO websites and invited the industries to respond to it."

The first company to have shown interest in making a full satellite was Zee Media which more than a decade ago pushed hard but it simply failed to take off possibly Zee Media was way ahead of its time. Today private players like Team Indus are making satellites in the private sector and in fact Team Indus is attempting to put a satellite around the moon, land an unmanned aircraft of the lunar surface and put a small buggy or a rover on the surface of the moon. A tall task for an Indian start-up but then nothing gets done without having big dream. Other Indian companies attempting to make small satellites are Dhruva Space and Sat Sure.

Earlier this year a space symposium organised by the Observer Research Foundation in New Delhi noted that "leading market research studies project that more than 1,800 satellites will be ordered and launched over the next decade, generating around $300 billion across global markets. India could capture a significant share of this expanding global space industry through greater involvement of its private sector entities. It has inherent advantages like the availability of skilled workforce, a stable and business-friendly government, positive investor climate, and low cost of operations. Initiatives such as 'Make in India' only reinforce the call for greater commercialisation of the industry. With 'New Space' start-ups emerging out of India, this sector has the potential to emerge as the third technological success front following the successes of the Information Technology and Biotechnology."

But all is not hunky-dory, the industry is also very apprehensive about tying up with ISRO since the deep wounds of the Antrix-Devas fiasco are still raw. ISRO was accused of crony capitalism when it was alleged that scarce S-band spectrum worth over ₹ 2 lakh crores was literally palmed off to Devas Multimedia Private Limited by ISRO. The commercial arm of ISRO Antrix Corporation lost its battle in Supreme Court to stall an international arbitration and subsequently the international arbitration also went against Antrix. Today, the government has initiated probe against retired officials of ISRO and against the owners of Devas. This prolonged commercial dispute does not augur well for India's space agency which is now trying to woo the private players. The old dictum once bitten twice shy may just keep the best of best private players from making the final leap. It would be in ISRO's interest to settle the Antrix-Devas case as early as possible so that confidence is built back in what people call a 'squeaky clean' organisation.

As it is often said space is a risky business and certainly not meant for the faint hearted now that ISRO has thrown open its doors looking for commercial partners, now it is the turn of the Indian industry to rise and shine and reach for the stars.

July 3, 2016

□

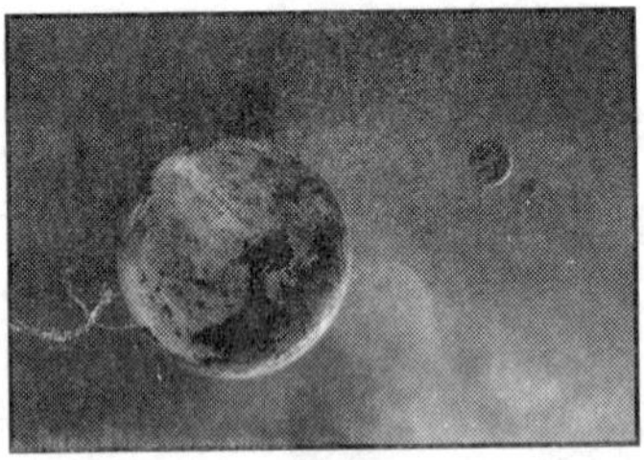

45

ISRO in Service of the Indian Soldier and the Indian War Machine

The precision 'surgical strikes' that Indian soldiers carried out on terrorist camps across the line of control were ably assisted and facilitated by metallic birds flying high in the sky unseen by Pakistanis, at least half a dozen satellites helped prepare and execute the precision strike.

India is fast developing a huge capability called 'C4ISR' or command, control, communications, computers, intelligence, surveillance, and reconnaissance. The country has already put in place an Aerospace Command and experts who understand the nature of the 'surgical strikes' acknowledge that this new tri-services body played a key role in planning and execution of the midnight attacks.

The Indian space agency the Indian Space Research Organisation (ISRO) evidently does not fight wars and is purely a civilian agency, but the capabilities it imparts to the nation are among the very best in world. From watching over with an eagle eye the terrorist and militant infrastructure in Pakistan to providing two-way communication in desolate places to giving out accurate navigation signals, ISRO has built a formidable infrastructure that helps India protects its borders in day or night. Not many Indians know of these deep capabilities that lie hidden within the portals of the space agency as ISRO's missions to Mars and Moon hog the lime light, but silently and steadily the 17000 strong workforce of ISRO contributes to keeping the lives of 1.2 billion Indians secure.

ISRO provides the necessary platforms, and then it is the user agencies that utilise its downstream products which means ISRO does not directly participate in the conflict. K. Kasturirangan former Chairman of ISRO says "the space agency has a formidable suit of technologies and all are suitably deployed with each user agency utilizing the assets to their best advantage". So a high resolution imaging satellite can help in urban planning while it can also monitor terrorist camps across the border. Kasturirangan says a satellite image does not distinguish between friend and foe that interpretation rests with the users.

Nobody doubts that ISRO's eyes and ears facilitated 'surgical strike' in Pakistan-occupied Kashmir at the staging points for terrorists. In years to come the role India's space assets will play a much bigger role if and when hostilities break out on our borders. Kiran Kumar, Chairman of ISRO says "the Indian space agency will not be found lacking in helping secure India's national interests now and in future".

Today, India has 33 satellites in orbit around the earth and one in the Martian orbit. These include 12 communications satellites; seven navigation satellites; 10 earth observation satellites and four weather monitoring satellites. This is one of the largest constellation of satellites in the Asia-Pacific region. Each bird is tailor-made for a specific purpose and each when needed helps protects India's supreme national interests.

India has some of the sharpest eyes in the sky and to prepare for the 'surgical strikes' India's best bird in the sky the Cartosat 2-series satellite launched as recently as June 22 played a key role. From its 526 kilometre perch this bird can peer at every object in Pakistan and can easily count the number of cars parked in the grand mansion of Pakistani Prime Minister Nawaz Sharif. With its almost 0.65 meter resolution as it rotates the earth every 90 minutes this formidable spy in the sky can count each and every tank, truck and fighter aircraft parked anywhere in Pakistan or for that matter anywhere India desires.

Speaking about the capabilities of this ultrasharp satellite Kumar said "the Cartosat-2 series has a unique capability of capturing a 1-minute video, which despite its enormous speed of 37 kms a second, is able to focus at a single point for a minute." In addition there were three other earth imaging satellites Cartosat-1, Cartosat-2 and Resourcesat-2 that provide top class imagery during day time. Going further ISRO seeks to develop satellites that have a resolution of 25 centimetres in the very near future.

In contrast, Pakistan has no such capability as its space program has hardly lifted off. G. Madhavan Nair former Chairman ISRO says even China does not have such high resolution satellites, the best China has is about five meter resolution. Nair says "India invested heavily in space imaging technology and is now reaping the benefits".

India also flies some satellites that have day and night viewing capabilities these are called the synthetic aperture radar satellites. There are two in orbit the RISAT-1 and RISAT-2. Nothing can hide from these mean birds as they can see through cloud cover and are not blinded at night. Especially, RISAT-2 is among the best in its class and its revisit time is relatively short. Assessing damage inflected on the camps that harboured the terrorists would be relatively easy using the radar satellites. It is not that these satellites don't help civilian activities, radar satellites help monitor floods and have even been deployed to search for crashed planes and helicopters.

India has recently put in place a regional satellite navigation system called NAVIC as recently as April

28, 2016 the last of the seven satellites was launched and Prime Minister Narendra Modi spoke elegantly on its huge benefits. This system gives the better than 20 meter accuracy for navigation signals akin to the American Global Positioning System (GPS) in an envelope which extends about 1500 kilometres from the border on all sides. The signals are being beamed down 24x7 all the year around. Only America and Russia have similar capability over the South Asian region, China is still putting in place its satellite navigation system.

The restricted signal which is available to the Indian armed forces is supposed to be even more accurate than the American GPS in the Indian region. Experts say it is unlikely that the Indian special forces used the hand-held devices from NAVIC to guide them to the terrorist camps as the devices are still being fine-tuned. India's enemies should have no doubts that very soon these *swadeshi* GPS signals will be leading India's commandos into the very den of master minds who control the terrorists. In an event of an all out war signals from NAVIC will undoubtedly help India target its whole suite of missiles to unleash unprecedented punishment on the enemy. Since the satellite navigation system is in India's control there can never be any fear of someone switching the constellation off.

There is another over 2000 kilogram bird that points towards the Indian region all day and night and provides unprecedented capability to India's armed forces. This is a satellite called GSAT-6 and this unique satellite has multi-media capability as it can stream video in both directions. It has the largest antennae which is six meter in diameter. This is one unique satellite which will play a crucial role in the network centric warfare of the 21st century.

Using a hand-held device individual soldiers can connect and will be able to transmit live pictures of what they can see from their helmet-mounted cameras even as they engage in combat. Launched last year the users are still developing the hand-held devices that can be made portable and compatible with this capability. Very soon this satellites twin GSAT 6-A may be flown which will have even more powerful capabilities. Nair says "the government and ISRO should expedite development of GSAT 6-A to have special capabilities that the special forces need". If one recalls in 2011 it was shown that President Barrack Obama monitored live feeds of the surgical strike the US carried out as part of Operation Geronimo to eliminate Osama Bin Laden in Pakistan. India's GSAT-6 and GSAT 6-A both will in principle be able to help providing live signals from the remotest of remote places in India's neighbourhood.

Sources in India's Aerospace Command confirm that they did have access to a live feed that was put in place using typical Indian *'jugaad'* but with these satellites such capabilities will become common place. Nair says right now India relies heavily on using Thuraya handsets for satellite telephony but he hopes very soon the Defence Research and Development Organisation (DRDO) will be able to deliver Indian handsets that are compatible with the country's GSAT-6 satellite. In fact, Nair insists that in the upcoming GSAT 6-A, satellite telephony should be made the bigger component.

While understandably much of the resources are focused on land since India has hostile neighbours both on its western and eastern fronts. ISRO has not forgotten the deep blue oceans that surround India and they need to be protected as well. On a specific demand by the Indian Navy, the Indian space scientists have already deployed a satellite the Navy calls 'Rukmini'. This is a dedicated communications satellite which helps the Indian Navy talk to its ships when they are beyond the visual range, in a secure fashion.

In coming years ISRO will also deliver a dedicated satellite made for the Indian Air Force. Prime Minister Narendra Modi is a known space buff who even monitors India's rocket launches even as he goes about executing his day-to-day parliamentary duties and he is well aware how and where to deploy India's space assets to make sure no one casts an evil eye on India.

Yet among all this one chink remains space infrastructure is very vulnerable to attacks of the star wars type. Hence having boots on the ground that can protect the boundary will always be necessary.

October 2, 2016

□

46
ISRO's French Connection

Indo-French love affair for rockets spans across Europe, Asia and South America. In faraway French Guiana at Kourou in South America housed in the middle of lush green rainforests is the expansive 700 square kilometre European space port. Least expecting when I reach there I encounter a heartening sight that fills one with national pride as I see the Indian tricolour hoisted alongside the French and European Union flags. Another fact makes me feel as if I am at home, is a poster announcing that I am in a zone that houses the deadly diseases like Dengue and Chikungunya to add to the icing it also warns against Zika. It is here that I find a band of about a dozen Indian aerospace scientists who had made a motel their temporary home and were carefully nurturing India's big bird the GSAT-18 satellite that was launched on the Ariane-5 rocket last week. Cooking their own meals of rasam and curd rice this merry gang kept a vigil on India's satellite as it rocketed over the Atlantic Ocean.

There is no other country other than France which has contributed and benefitted the most in partnering with India in the space sector. From helping India in its very first baby rocket launch way back in 1963 to having launched India's latest heavy weight communication satellite GSAT-18 on October 6, 2016, the Indo-French connection are deep and strong.

India and France have made rocket engines together,

helped each other learn things that were being denied to one another, have made satellites for each other and more than that both have helped train human resources in this frontier area. Today both countries are recognised as front line space powers each in their own right.

Not known to many India even contributed to the making and testing of the mighty Ariane rockets. On the 280th launch of rockets from Kourou and the seventy-fourth consecutively successful launch of the massive Ariane-5 rocket, India's GSAT-18 a 3404 kg communications satellite that helps the country boost its television and banking services was successfully placed in orbit.

ISRO Chairman A.S. Kiran Kumar, who watched the launch from the Jupiter building of the control centre in Kourou, called it "glorious and flawless mission and like on all previous occasions, Ariane space provided a magnificent textbook launch".

India has had a long association since 1983 with Arianespace and Centre National Détudes Spatiales (CNES) or the French space agency as Kumar says "this was the 20th launch for ISRO and we have been having a long co-operation with Ariane starting with our Ariane Passenger Payload Experiment (APPLE). At ISRO we have capability of putting only 2.2 tons in orbit and we come to Kourou and Ariane for putting higher capacity satellites." This twentieth launch was only the latest, in early years when the Ariane rocket was still struggling and had suffered back to back failures, it was India that risked putting its APPLE satellite a 350 kg communications satellite on-board the third launch of the Ariane-1 rocket in 1983. To be fair CNES provided India with a free launch and since then the gates for commerce in rocket launching using the Ariane family of rockets have not closed. In 2017, India hopes to launch another two heavy duty communication satellites GSAT-17 and GSAT-11 using the trusted Ariane-5 rocket.

In 1963 when ISRO was yet to be born, India launched its first sounding rocket from Thumba, a Nike Apache rocket given by the Americans, but even in this first launch the French link was evident as the payload of the sodium vapour experiment was provided by France.

Legendary French aerospace scientist Jacques Blamont was present at hand on November 21, 1963 in the fishing village of Thumba in Kerala who says "he had no difficulty convincing CNES to provide a radar for tracking and the sodium payloads to be placed first on the first sounding rocket". Blamont recalls that "a young engineer was sent the night before to fit the payload and nose cone, he later became the President of India in Dr. A.P.J. Abdul Kalam".

One of ISRO workhorse liquid fuelled rocket engines is the Vikas motor that still flies on both the Polar Satellite Launch Vehicle (PSLV) and the Geosynchronous Satellite Launch Vehicle (GSLV) also has its origins in France. According to Blamont, "for India, the really major breakthrough in liquid propulsion systems came in 1974 when ISRO signed an agreement with the Société Européenne de Propulsion (SEP) located in Vernon, France. At that time the French were developing the Viking liquid engine for their Ariane launch vehicle program. Without any exchange of funds, this agreement provided for technology transfer from SEP to ISRO for the Viking liquid engine. In return, ISRO would spare the services of 100 man-years of ISRO engineers and scientists to SEP for their Ariane launch vehicle development. Forty engineers, with a five years contract, participated in the technology acquisition program in France". This is the real beginning of the success story of the Indian and French rockets.

In more recent times India has launched some of Europe's sharpest eyes in the skies in the form of Spot-6 and Spot-7 satellites a few years ago. That the French relied on India's highly reliable PSLV launcher shows how the two countries trust each other's capabilities.

In more recent times, the two jointly made a satellite dedicated to study the water cycle on Earth called Megha Tropiques. This is a 1000 kg earth imaging satellite and was launched using the PSLV in 2011. Just last week ISRO and CNES inked a new understanding to jointly continue with the mission for another four years. According to Mathieu Weiss, the CNES representative in India "the mission has already given rise to some 90 published scientific articles and more than 1,400 citations." Weiss adds that the mission is delivering a dynamic three-dimensional picture of different states of water in the atmosphere. The main feature of the satellite is the combination of its instruments and its position over the intertropical belt, in a lowinclination orbit enabling up to five revisits to the same location every day. This unique capability has allowed it to achieve remarkable progress in estimating rainfall and forecasting cyclones, monsoons and droughts. Continuous monitoring of the turbulent giant tropical convection spots, where most extreme weather phenomena form, provides a better understanding of the cycles affecting mid-latitude countries and is extremely valuable for the global climate science community.

Forging a new partnership CNES and ISRO have decided to engage in new joint climate missions. The French Argos datacollection instrument will fly on the Indian Oceansat-3 satellite in 2018. France and India have also begun development of a future joint thermal infrared observation satellite.

"India is one of the best partners and customers for France" says CNES President Jean-Yves Le Gall who says in times to come ISRO and CNES can hopefully jointly explore planets like Venus and Mars where India is already planning missions. Blamont wants India and France to jointly launch an orbiter to Venus that will then send balloons down into the little understood atmosphere of the Venus.

"After India's Mars Orbiter Mission (MOM), the next step has to be a lander. A lander on Mars is not easy, but it will be interesting to undertake," says Le Gall and earlier this year on India's Republic Day at the summit meeting between India and France a letter of intent was indeed inked to explore landing on Mars.

In space technology, no frontier is impossible and no dream is too big for India and France as they soar ever higher to decipher the unknowns of the universe, while not forgetting the needs of earthlings.

October 16, 2016

□

47

Moon Shot Politics: Will an Indian Start-up 'Tea Indus' Beat ISRO in Planting India's Flag on the Moon?

Move over China, the Asian space race has been overtaken by a new race to the moon, taking place this time right in the heart of Bengaluru. A massive dash to reach the moon between a 'David' being played by Team Indus and the big 'Goliath' the Indian Space Research Organisation (ISRO).

Both want to reach the moon within 60 days of each other. ISRO has the wisdom and heritage and Team Indus the young nervous energy and a spirit to burn out and die fighting. Team Indus aims to hoist India's flag through an unmanned spacecraft on the lunar surface on January 26, 2018, the 69th Republic Day of India.

Team Indus is a group of youngsters who are hedging their bets on winning the $20 million Google Lunar X Prize. Team Indus comprises about 100 people mostly engineers and are led by a visionary Team Leader Rahul Narayan who in his earlier *avatar* was a software worker and calls himself a serial entrepreneur but who in 2010 when the Google Prize Lunar X Prize was almost closing decided to take shot at the moon. Team Indus is the only Indian team in this Google-sponsored global effort. Narayan says they have personally explained the mission to India's top space buff Prime Minister Narendra Modi who has extended his blessings to the young team.

Since 2010 Narayan has collected a bunch youngsters mostly, fresh out of college students who have made it their single-minded desire to become the first private Indian company to reach the moon. Team Indus has roped in angel investors like Nandan Nilekani and Ratan Tata and space sages like Dr. K. Kasturirangan as advisors and have till date managed to garner some ₹ 100 crores in funding for a total expected mission cost of about ₹ 400 crores. Narayan confirms they have already spent the first one hundred crores.

To make up for the thin experience in flying to distances as far as 400,000 kilometres away the founders of Team Indus have recruited some two dozen retired hands from ISRO who provide the necessary brain that the young brawn ably provides.

Team Indus has just procured a launch services agreement with Antrix Corporation Ltd the commercial arm of ISRO to source India's highly reliable Polar Satellite Launch Vehicle or PSLV. Rakesh Sasibhushan, Chairman-cum-Managing Director, Antrix Corporation, Bengaluru confirms that "yes we have signed a launch services agreement with Team Indus which essentially provides a PSLV launch for launching a lunar orbiter and lander sometime in the fourth quarter of 2017". This is for the very first time ISRO is making what it calls "a precious national resource in PSLV", available albeit at a still undisclosed cost to a private Indian company.

As part of the Google Lunar X Prize competition which after an extension of two deadlines is likely to end by 2017 before which all the competing teams which number about three dozen have to kick off their moon shot. As off now one Israeli team and two American teams have procured launch contracts and are close contenders for the prize.

Towards what Team Indus calls *'Har Indian Ka Moonshot'* in the next 12 months it has to build from scratch a satellite that will lift off from India's space port Sriharikota atop riding on the PSLV, the same then has to make a soft landing on the moon and then a rover will have to slip out. To finally win the prize the rules stipulate that the rover has to move 500 meters on the lunar surface and should be able to beam back high definition images back to earth.

Team Indus claims they are now among the top four contenders for the prize and they already bagged $1 million milestone prize from Google. This has buoyed their spirits and today among the half a dozen other serious contenders only Team Indus has a 'verified contract' to launch on a highly reliable globally acclaimed rocket.

Vivek Raghavan, lead for technology at Team Indus also called Jedi Master (Tech)—bringing an aura of a Star Wars like setting—says "as part of the Google Lunar X Prize, there are obviously many teams in the beginning. There are still 16 teams in the competition. But the number of teams that actually have a launch contract are very few. We've been ranked among the top three teams in the world in the competition."

In contrast, ISRO has been plodding along since 2008 with its much anticipated *Chandrayaan-2* mission a massive exercise to indigenously make an orbiter, a soft lander and a rover that will be blasted into space according to Dr. Jitendra Singh the Minister for Space Affairs in the Prime Minister's Office in the first quarter of 2018. ISRO is hoping to deploy its heavy weight launcher the Geosynchronous Satellite Launch Vehicle (GSLV) which has had a rather patchy record and was dubbed by ISRO as its 'naughty boy' for this prestigious mission.

Chandrayaan-2 is a heavy weight over 3000 kilogram satellite in comparison Team Indus's puny satellite weighing

600 kg baby, but with broadly similar goals. Truly, a race between a truck and a Nano!

Rahul Narayan says ISRO and Team Indus are not competitors in the unfolding 'Indian moon race'. He likens "Team Indus to be playing a Twenty-twenty cricket match as against ISRO playing full-fledged Test match with *Chandrayaan-2*".

Some soothing words from A.S. Kiran Kumar, Chairman, ISRO who in a statement to Team Indus said "if you treat space as the new frontier, then who better than the next generation of people who bring in new innovative approaches. We want to see there is enough capacity to make use of the knowledge in India for the world market."

For Team Indus the launch window starts on 28, December, 2017, the PSLV will inject the spacecraft into an orbit 880 km × 70,000 km around the Earth. The spacecraft will then undertake a soft land in Mare Imbrium, a region in the North-Western hemisphere of the Moon. Narayan adds "we have a very young team and I must say we've got a bright bunch of folks here. We've managed to break down the problem to many pieces and till date we've done reasonably well. We've had a few failures, but I think we've had more success than failures. In addition to our young team, we obviously have several retired ISRO scientists who are architects of what we're building today. It is a challenging task, but I think we set out to be able to build the spacecraft."

But now that ISRO has positioned itself and given a green signal for Team Indus to use the PSLV a rocket that in its heritage has the 2008 *Chandrayaan-1* launch can the upstart team from Bengaluru expect a cake walk to the rocket port. When asked if ISRO was taking a risk by allowing an inexperienced player to launch on the PSLV Sasibhushan, said "not really, all satellites that have to fly on the PSLV have to undergo a qualification test and we will ensure that the [Team Indus] satellite is worthy of flying on the PSLV and unless it passes all tests we will not be able to fly it in PSLV".

In 2008 India fought and lost a marathon race to reach the moon against China when *Chandrayaan-1* lost out to China's maiden mission to the moon Chang'e-1, the Indian Government never really pardoned ISRO for that loss of face. ISRO is still smarting on having lost in becoming the first Asian nation to reach the lunar orbit so will it be large hearted to let an Indian start-up once again take lead in placing India's flag on the moon.

Watch this space as two energized 'lunatic' Bengaluru teams keep their eyes glued on that parched white ball the Moon in this new game of planetary cricket.

December 4, 2016

□

48

Troubles from Neighbours Make India and Israel Forge Friendly Ties in Space

India and Israel today survive against huge odds in a very hostile neighbourhood, in an effort to find suitable solutions to contain the very fountainheads that spur terrorism, the two countries will jointly explore using space technologies as a counter measure to thwart the menace of terrorism while also meeting the civilian applications of space. Both Jerusalem and New Delhi have deep strengths space technology. Born within the same year both have to spend massive amounts of money to secure their borders from neighbours who are hell bent in fomenting trouble for the civilian populations.

The heads of the Israel Space Agency (ISA) and the Indian Space Research Organisation (ISRO) met this week in Bengaluru to draw up a roadmap of cooperation in this high technology sector. If all goes well early in 2017 two Israeli Nano-satellites will also be launched from Sriharikota.

Avi Blasberger the Director General of the Israel Space Agency (ISA) confirmed that one key area of cooperation being explored is 'remote sensing using microwaves'. This is essentially a technology where special birds called RadarSats are deployed that have the built-in capability of day and night surveillance and these eyes in the skies can even see through overcast cloudy skies, giving the enemy little room to hide. In common parlance, this sophisticated technology is often termed as 'spy satellites' since one can keep a track of one's enemy 24×7 in all weather conditions.

It is no secret that both Prime Minister Narendra Modi and Prime Minister of Israel Benjamin Netanyahu have a mutual fan club and both have respect for each other's styles of governance. Blasberger said the "environment between the two countries is very good and joint projects and joint space missions could be a big possibility".

Israel has some of the best radar imaging technology and in 2008, India launched on behalf of Israel a satellite called TecSAR. This small 295 kilogram satellite was successfully placed in orbit using India's Polar Satellite Launch Vehicle (PSLV) launched from Sriharikota. Israel lacked an indigenous rocket that could launch a satellite of this nature and India's east facing rocket port is ideally suited with a flight path that goes over oceans as against the Israeli rocket port.

This TecSAR reconnaissance satellite has the capability of mapping object at a resolution of less than a meter from its perch some 500 kilometres above earth. This eye in the sky reports suggest helped Israel map the military capabilities of its hostile neighbours. It was considered one of the most advanced spy satellites of its kind.

Later India also procured from Israel a similar satellite which New Delhi named RISAT-2. In 2009, this 300 kg special beast that could track as some reports suggest objects as small as 10 centimetres was hoisted into space using the PSLV. This satellite from its 400 kilometre orbit has been actively used by India to monitor activities in camps across the border in Pakistan to thwart infiltration bids by terrorists. Experts says images from RISAT-2 helped in India launching the 'surgical strikes' across the line of control this year that resulted in Indian military annihilating several 'terrorist launch pads' in Pakistan-occupied Kashmir.

Both countries have indeed secured their borders using these special microwave imaging satellites. Blasberger for the first time confirmed that "the space agencies of the two countries were not directly involved", in India launching the Israeli satellite 'TecSAR' and in India procuring its clone RISAT-2. Blasberger said both ISA and ISRO work in the area of supporting the civilian programs.

Blasberger said "Israel will be happy to provide more RISAT-2 type reconnaissance satellites to India" if New Delhi made a request. But what is most significant is that the two countries have now set up a special working group to enhance and explore how best 'microwave imaging' can help both countries. India has also developed and launched its own special Radar imaging satellite called RISAT-1. It may be noted that radar satellites are also very helpful in mapping floods and other agriculture-related activities.

Blasberger said "Israel has special capabilities in fabricating precision cameras and miniaturisation of space equipment", on the other hand he felt India has highly developed rockets that can deploy heavy satellites in space. This 'complementarity' can be a win-win for both countries which have advanced space technologies at their disposal says Blasberger.

The heads of two space agencies have also agreed to set up joint teams that would explore how to build bridges between the two space fairing nations in cutting edge areas like 'electrical propulsion, remote sensing and communications'.

Rather upbeat after his visit to some of the ISRO facilities in Bengaluru, Blasberger felt "working together will cultivate more work for the future". It seems hostile neighbours on earth is forcing India and Israel to join hands in space to secure their future.

December 11, 2016

□

49

Touching Lives: ISRO's Space Technology can Save Lives of Soldiers at the Siachen Glacier

The bigger killer on the heights of the Siachen Glacier is not the enemy bullets from the Pakistan Army but the extreme weather. Fewer soldiers would die if some of the technologies developed by the Indian Space Research Organisation (ISRO) for use in space were quickly and effectively deployed for protecting our soldiers. ISRO has developed the world's lightest insulating material and also a high-powered search and rescue beacon technologies that can touch and save lives of Indian soldiers serving on the world's highest battleground.

In the last three years, at least 41 soldiers have lost their lives at the Siachen glacier according to the Ministry of Defence. Since 1984, when India occupied the icy heights, about 1000 soldiers have died on the Siachen glacier and as per the official records, only 220 of these have been felled by enemy bullets. At those heights of 6000-7000 meters, extreme weather is the bigger killer. If only our soldiers get access to some of the latest developments from Indian labs, many lives could be saved. Then there is lethargy on both sides. Scientists find it hard to transfer technology to the industry and the industry complains that half-baked products are passed on. Hence, the failure rate is very high.

Despite upgrades, Indian soldiers still wear very heavy clothes. Now scientists at ISRO have developed an ultra-light weight material that acts as an effective insulator. Another game changer could be the hand-held search and rescue radio signal emitter that can be detected by satellites. This can help effectively pinpoint the location of soldiers lost or buried in avalanches.

Dr. K. Sivan, well-known rocket scientist and Director of the Vikram Sarabhai Space Centre (VSSC) in Thiruvananthapuram, says with a little tweaking these materials and technologies developed for hi-tech space applications can easily be spun off for societal use. Sivan says 'ISRO uses tax payer money. So, it is answerable to the Indian public'. ISRO's rockets and satellites certainly help lay people but there are many more developments hidden in the 'temples of technology' like the VSSC that can be used to help save lives.

If some of these technologies were being used, possibly Lance Naik Hanamanthappa Koppad and the nine other soldiers who lost their lives earlier this year at the Siachen Glacier could well have been saved. If only these soldiers were using clothing made of the 'silica aerogel', they may possibly have been saved from freezing to death. Similarly, if the soldiers were equipped with suitable hand-held 'search and rescue' devices, their location could have been easily pin-pointed using Indian satellites and rescue efforts could have been speeded up.

ISRO Masters World Lightest Material

Recently, India's main lab that specialises in making rockets for the country mastered the art of making the 'world's lightest artificial material' called 'silica aerogel'. This aerogel is actually a solid but within its complex matrix, it encapsulates 99% air. This gives it several unique properties. It is incredibly light, it is a great thermal insulator. Dr. Naga Priya, a scientist in Advanced Materials & Ceramics Division at VSSC, who is part of the team that made this material, explains 'that the process to make the silica aerogel is highly guarded'. So, standardising the procedure to make the aerogel took her team a lot of effort. The team hopes to use some of the 'silica aerogel' for insulating the tanks that hold the liquid hydrogen and liquid oxygen in the cryogenic engines. Since it is light-weight, it could also be used in designing the space suits that future Indian astronauts may be wearing. The small buggy that will be part of the Chandrayaan-2 and will run around the lunar surface in 2018 could also see the use of the 'silica aerogel' as an insulator. Naga Priya explains her lab is already in discussion with the Indian Ordinance Factory that manufactures clothes for the soldiers to see how this new material can be sandwiched between layers of cloth for making light-weight parkas, socks and gloves for the soldiers who are posted at the Siachen Glacier.

The Indian space scientists have already made small pieces of the silica aerogel that resemble a fabric but still it is very fragile and suitable fabric has to be developed that can effectively sandwich this great insulator.

There are other societal benefits of using the 'silica aerogel'. If window panes are given a coating of this new material, light would come easily but heat would be contained, says Naga Priya. She says imagine a building, whose exterior is coated with this top-class insulator, the building would be cool in summer and warm in winter. Reducing the load on air conditioning could lead to the saving of a lot electricity and help combat climate change.

It is not that the material is fully ready to be deployed for all these varied uses. It is still very expensive to make and some of it is very fragile. The team at VSSC uses evaporation at ambient temperature to make some of the aerogels. This is cheaper than the specialised super critical drying technique used to make aerogels for special applications. There are many industrial applications like in furnaces where these special materials can also be easily used.

Satellite-aided Search and Rescue

Scientists at ISRO have developed small portable devices that can help in search and rescue. There are hand-held devices that can be carried by trekkers and soldiers when they traverse the desolate regions. These smart devices can be activated using a button and once initiated, they emit a radio beacon that can be detected by satellites. Using the Global Positioning System (GPS), the exact location of the person who is in distress can be automatically pin-pointed. The battery-powered device sends up a signal, which can then be automatically tracked at ground stations in Lucknow and Bengaluru. If only Lance Naik Hanumanthappa were carrying this device, his rescue could have been greatly speeded up.

A similar but slightly larger device has been made by VSSC for use by fishermen. This can be fitted on the fishing boats and it can either be triggered manually or when it encounters salt water, it gets triggered. This device transmits a pulsed signal in the 406 MHz band and it can help in locating ships lost at sea. The batteries are robust enough to transmit a signal for at least 65 hours at a stretch. ISRO has helped save the lives of many trekkers in the Himalayas and is eager to help the Indian armed forces in case they seek to use the device at the remote locations in times of emergency.

Portable Fuel Cell Power Generator

Ensuring uninterrupted maintenance-free power supply at remote locations is a nightmare for technologists. Now the scientists at VSSC have made a portable fuel cell system that can produce electricity directly from fuels through an electrochemical process where the only inputs needed are hydrogen gas and air. Based on the 'proton exchange membrane' technology, the gadget made at VSSC can generate up to about 100 watts of power. This is like lighting a single bulb but then there are several small devices that need only a small amount of power for it to work round the clock. An all-weather automatic weather station powered using this indigenously made fuel cell is currently being tested at Dehradun. Another digital Global Positioning System device has been deployed at the Gangotri Glacier to see how this hydrogen-powered device works at high altitudes. There are also plans to use the sophisticated G-SAT-6 satellite's multimedia communication capability to deploy surveillance systems in remote locations from where Pakistani infiltrators creep into Indian territory and make devastating terrorist attacks on India. Such automatic remotely operated cameras could be powered using the maintenance-free 'fuel cells' and then they could beam pictures up to the Indian satellites through which soldiers could maintain a 24x7 vigil from far away. This would be akin to having closed circuit television (CCTV) cameras but in places where there is neither power supply nor continuous human presence.

Sivan says a suitable industrial partners are being actively identified and the technologies will be transferred so that the so-called 'rocket science' no longer remains rocket science. More importantly, he says 'desi technology' can be used to power the 'Make in India' effort and help save lives.

April 03, 2016

□

50

Big gains for ISRO under Modi. 'Achchhe Din and a Naya Savera' for the Indian space community as NAVIC was navigated into place

Two years of Prime Minister Narendra Modi have seen some 'achhe din' (good days) and a 'naya savera' (new dawn) for the Indian space agency. Since Modi took over India's spaceship reached planet Mars, the successful launch of India's mini space shuttle India was spectacular. ISRO kick-started the classic swadeshi satellite-based navigation system. Towards the end of this year, ISRO is now getting ready to launch the unique South Asia Satellite, a friendly communications satellite for the South Asian neighbours, actually conceived by Modi himself. The launch of India's first space observatory AstroSAT that gives India's scientists a unique view of the universe also fructified successfully.

Most importantly, Modi pushed for use of space-based technologies in day-to-day governance of India, where he sat through two hours of open grilling of line ministry secretary-level bureaucrats on how they plan to use space assets.

Two years of the Prime Minister Narendra Modi government have seen classic turnaround for the Indian Space Research Organisation (ISRO). During the Prime

Minister Manmohan Singh government, the 'squeaky clean' space agency was scorched by the worst scandal of this century dubbed the Devas-Antrix S-band spectrum scandal, where a total of upwards of ₹ two lakh crores was allegedly swindled through crony dealings. The morale at the space agency hit rock bottom but it did not lose focus.

On May 26, 2014, when Modi took over, little did people know that the former 'chaiwallah' was an ardent space buff. Modi vibes well with the chairman of ISRO, Dr. Kiran Kumar with whom he has interacted since his days in Ahmedabad when Modi was chief minister of Gujarat and Kiran Kumar was head of the Space Applications Centre there. Kumar has spent close to four decades working in Gujarat and manages to speak a smattering of Gujarati as well. The good chemistry has helped ISRO.

In the last two years, under special instruction from Modi, the Indian space agency made a very special dash to complete India's NAVIC – "Navigation with Indian Constellation", when the last of the seven satellites was successfully placed in the orbit by the Polar Satellite Launch Vehicle on April 28, 2016. During Modi's tenure in rapid succession, five of the seven satellites of NAVIC were put in orbit. The Indian satellite constellation is already providing day and night coverage of the navigation signal throughout the Indian region. This is a unique achievement by ISRO.

Modi took forward a germ of an idea from former Prime Minister Atal Bihari Vajpayee's tenure, when during the Kargil conflict, India was denied access to the best quality satellite-based navigation system signals it desperately sought to annihilate with pin-point accuracy the reinforced bunkers on the high hills made by the Pakistanis. The first round of the National Democratic Alliance government laid the foundation for the swadeshi GPS which Modi has fulfilled.

Other than India, globally, satellite-based navigational

signals over South Asia are provided only by the American constellation of the Global Positioning System (GPS) and the Russian constellation that uses a system called GLONASS. It is ISRO's claim that the Indian navigation system is superior to both these systems for the South Asian region. Moreover, the American and Russian systems use 4 times as many satellites for their systems, making NAVIC (like a lot of ISRO's technology) very frugal, operating with just 7 satellites. It must, of course, be clarified that the Indian NAVIC provides a regional signal while the American and Russian systems have global footprints. When required, India's footprint can also be made global by augmenting the number of satellites.

NAVIC's assured signal coverage extends over the country and about 1,500 kilometres beyond Indian borders, and experts explain the rationale for this as being based on the current threat perception that exists for the country.

NAVIC – working for both the average and more specialised user – beams down two types of signals. First, signals that can be tapped by the average user on any compatible smart phone, with accuracy on this frequency better than 20 metres, according to ISRO. Second, special, highly accurate signals for usage largely by India's security establishments to make sure that India's borders are well protected (the "restricted users"). The NAVIC satellite navigation system has cost the Indian government close to ₹ 1400 crore.

Today, in 2016, India holds the distinction of being the third country to have such a robust system over South Asia. Despite a late start, ISRO completed the deployment of the NAVIC system in a record 3 years. This significant milestone has been reached under the leadership of Modi.

It was just in 2013 when the first of the seven satellites in this constellation was launched. It was understood that India was the sixth country to initiate efforts for its own satellite-based navigation system with USA, Russia, European Union, Japan and China all actively pushing the frontier on satellite-based navigation systems. Then the Americans and Russians took more than a decade to complete their work.

According to India's Science and Technology Minister, Dr. Harsh Vardhan, India initiated this effort upon the denial of access to such signals during the Kargil conflict. Vardhan shared his pride about the great display of skill and capability of the Indian science and technology establishment – with such a completely Made-in-India effort for the people of this country.

To make sure that the point is driven home that he keeps a hawk's eye on the Department of Space, Modi witnessed live the launching of the seventh and last satellite in the Indian Regional Navigation Satellite System (IRNSS) from his office in the South Block. He also spoke spontaneously about ways in which such a system could be used by India's people. It was Modi who christened the system NAVIC, which means 'sailor' in Hindi. He described how these brave men from India's glorious past would navigate the sea using stars, adding with pride that ISRO's new star would make for easier navigation.

Modi also built on what seems to be an initiative close to his heart – of working on India's immediate neighbours and strengthening these ties, and said that NAVIC's services could be offered to the country's South Asian neighbours. Modi said: "With this successful launch, we will determine our own paths powered by our technology. This is a great gift to people from scientists." He described this as an example of "Make in India" and "Made for Indians".

There are already a select few compatible smart phones that are receiving NAVIC signals and, apparently, all Indian handsets will be made compatible using chipsets that are enabled to receive signals from NAVIC.

In an India increasingly digital, the idea of Indian entrepreneurs using more and more Indian signals is indeed an attractive one. Dependency on foreign vendors for providing satellite-based navigation systems may also reduce and eventually cease, increasing self-sustained resilience.

Navigating road routes as one travels through the country, or increased efficiency of deployment of the transportation sector, or monitoring the movement of trains in the vast Indian railways network, NAVIC's signals would be put to great use in the future. There is little doubt that this would streamline road, rail and ship transport, also making it cheaper and more cost-efficient. There is a hope that these signals may help improve women's safety, based on the usage of distress or panic signals using the panic button that are to be introduced on all Indian mobile phone handsets by 2018.

The now-famous frugal and effective engineering model that ISRO excels in has once again come out a winner, helping large goals like securing Indian borders, but also perhaps providing an impetus to the Indian economy and under Modi, it has got a new energy and zeal to fulfil the aspirations of the 1.25 billion people. Perhaps reaching for the stars is just the beginning of India's quest to master and domesticate outer space.

June 12, 2016

□□□